HEALING *the* PAIN *of* HEARTACHE

Praise for Dr. Erv Hinds's
Healing the Pain of Heartache

"Dr. Hinds has expertly described a phenomenon that many of us in health care have observed but has been poorly understood—the intersection between emotion and the biology of heartache. In doing so, he makes a substantial contribution to the field of medicine and provides practical guidance to those who treat or have experienced this universal pain." *Fred N. Davis, MD*, Co-Founder, Michigan Pain Consultants; Assistant Clinical Professor, Michigan State University College of Human Medicine, Grand Rapids, Michigan.

"This book is filled with profound wisdom and guidance offering a future of hope for those suffering loss. The personal experience of a wounded healer speaks to the unmet needs of those suffering from sickness and loss and provides a road map to assist in navigating the journey to recovery. The wisdom expressed in this book can bring a deeper satisfaction to physicians, at any stage in life, through seeking the path of healing in their own practice." *Dick Lueker, MD*, Cardiologist, Albuquerque, New Mexico.

"*Healing the Pain of Heartache* is on the one hand a medical manual about heartache, and on the other an inspirational tool to navigate through the pain of heartache. It is a magnificent resource. Erv Hinds legitimizes the diagnosis of 'heartache' medically, emotionally, and spiritually…but more importantly through his personal story and the stories of his patients, he challenges all of us to sit in silence with our self, a friend, or a professional and allow ourselves to heal the pain of heartache." *Carolyn Silver*, **Rabbi**, Santa Fe, New Mexico. Carolyn Silver received her degree at Yale Divinity School and was non-traditionally ordained as a rabbi in 1992. She had a twenty-eight year career in hospice and now is in her sixth year as an energy medicine practitioner.

HEALING *the* PAIN *of* HEARTACHE

A Physician Explores Broken Heart Syndrome

ERV HINDS, MD

Also by Erv Hinds, MD

A Life Larger than Pain

CONTENTS

FOR

Eric, Emily, and Ellie

Preface

WHY READ THIS BOOK?

This book provides medical evidence underlying our intuitive knowledge of heartache. We all want evidence-based medicine when we're in the emergency room, but we also want recognition of how emotional suffering can affect physical well-being.

I've been practicing medicine for over forty years—from my service as commanding officer on a firebase in Vietnam to chairman of the intensive care unit of a first-rate private general hospital. I first learned about the intricacies of the heart in 1975 when I became an anesthesiologist for an open-heart surgical team in Albuquerque, New Mexico. It was a very scientific relationship with the heart that required balancing medications, blood pressure, oxygen, and carbon dioxide levels while the surgeons operated. Intense vigilance and rapid responses to physiological changes were essential.

Ten years later I received a personal education in heart repair as my own heart disease reached a life-threatening level. I had known that I had a defective mitral heart valve, but a chest x-ray revealed an enlarged heart. I was acutely aware that I would eventually develop heart failure if the valve defect were not corrected. Within months I underwent experimental heart valve repair (*not* valve replacement) in Paris, France. At the time, this was experimental surgery unavailable in the United States due to the medical malpractice climate. The surgery was successful, and my heart size returned to normal. For the past twenty-five years I have lived an active life with no restrictions.

The surgery allowed me to assume the role of the wounded healer. The grace I felt in the months leading up to, including, and following the surgery meant that my relationship with the heart moved from the concrete to the personal and, ultimately, to the spiritual level. This experience was so profound that it changed the way I interacted with patients and led me to change the emphasis of my practice from anesthesiology to pain management medicine.

Yet another wound to the heart occurred when my twenty-year-old daughter abruptly died in 2003. This devastating loss intimately acquainted me with the all-encompassing reality of heartache. I wondered why this emotional pain felt so very physical.

This book is neither a memoir of heartache nor a how-to manual for recovering from grief. There are many excellent books on grief and heartbreak that specifically target emotional recovery, and I recommend that you acquaint yourself with them if you are in need of practical help for working through a significant loss in your life. This book *is* intended to be a companion for such books by providing a medical perspective on heartache as a legitimate pain we need to treat, just as we would any other illness or physical pain. I will examine recovery holistically, as a complex cluster of physical, mental, emotional, and spiritual factors.

I hope you will consider this book a success if your benefits include:

- *Understanding how heartache acts upon the body to produce the profound changes scientifically documented in what is commonly called "broken heart syndrome."*
- *Validating the literal physicality of heartache—an acknowledgment that our pain and body knowledge is real, not just imagined.* Exposing the wounds of a broken heart gives us a mandate to seek healing, just as we would attend to any other physical or psychological trauma to body, mind, and spirit, including the scientific wisdom of evidence-based medicine.
- *Recognizing the possibility of severe consequences of a broken heart.* Both medical practitioners and patients should be alerted to the urgency of incorporating heartache into a medical work-up as a valid part of routine history. The simple question, "Are you currently experiencing a loss, grief, or heartache?" establishes this as an issue.
- *Rehabilitating a broken heart that has surrendered to helplessness.* The reality is that there is no going back to the way life was before the heartbreak, but rehab offers hope that heartache will no longer define us. Recognition and treatment of the broken heart can be more than an antidote as information and insight help us to develop new and healthier patterns of thought and behavior. The heart can grow less vulnerable to malfunction in the event of heartache.

Whether you are a medical professional or a heartache sufferer (or both), I hope this book will bring healing to some of the deepest wounds of the heart.

1

HOW AM I GOING
TO SURVIVE THIS PAIN?

Only rarely now do I stop and tell myself, incredulous,
"This must be a nightmare. It can't be real."
—Luci Shaw[1]

November 20, 2003. The phone rings at the Santa Fe Pain and
Spine Center at 5:45 a.m. It's the coroner of Las Vegas, Nevada.
He asks if I am Ervin Hinds, father of Elizabeth Allison Hinds.
He states that he has Ellie's body; she died at about 2:00 a.m.
He relays details of the death of my daughter in a cold, detached
way as I sink into physical shock and emotional loss—a hollow,
chilling, downdraft of despair.

Everything in the room seems gray and lifeless, including
me. Breathing is a conscious effort. I cup my arms and
hands around my head and drop onto the desk to hide from
this crushing reality; part of me is also dying. My heart is
pounding without purpose. Is this a living death by inches or

---

1   Luci Shaw, *God in the Dark: Through Grief and Beyond* (East *Sussex*, UK: Highland Books,
1990), p. 204.

a prodrome—a sign of death coming for me? I would almost welcome it to escape this injury to my spirit, this terrible heartache. Years of repressed anxiety, fear, and sadness bring a flood of tears. The wrenching sobs seem to empty my heart of any vital force to continue.

I feel darkness creep into the room. As in a dream, I long to escape—but I am disabled by a black grief that is way beyond sadness. It is a fatal injury to body and mind—I need physical and emotional life support.

November 20, 2004. I sit overlooking the West Fork of the San Juan River on the deck of our family home at the foot of Wolf Creek Pass, Colorado. One year has passed since the death of my daughter Ellie.

I function well at home and at work. I even laugh. But a hole in my heart remains—an irrevocable damage to my being. The perceived void stretches from my brain to my chest and to my soul. It sucks my thoughts, my energy, and my characteristically positive disposition down its dark tunnel. Modern medicine does not explain this sense of interconnectedness between body, mind, and spirit.

Each new day brings lingering traces of Ellie...memories aroused by another girl's wide-open smile so like hers...a sight, sound, or smell that triggers a cascade of memories that seem to be occurring *in the present.* Why do I let these reflections cover me with this gray feeling of despair? When will I be able to celebrate them as priceless and valuable?

What is the antidote to heartbreak? What is the pill or procedure to relieve this pain the sages say only time will heal—perhaps it will endure a lifetime.

As much as I long to be at the Wolf Creek retreat next to the river's untrammeled splendor, the house has an emptiness where Ellie used to lounge and laugh. Wherever she was, she filled the space with her exuberance and spontaneity— although she often flew far too close to the flame.

Anxiety had been with me for many years as I watched her high-risk behavior. But I had hoped for her to gain caution with maturity. In her last six months Ellie had told me that she'd enjoyed a wonderful childhood. So much of her joy had occurred at Wolf Creek among the wildlife, wildflowers, stream, and sky. We took horseback rides, restored the riverbed and riparian zones of our stretch of the San Juan, and observed the lessons revealed by nature. The wholesome times in Colorado contrasted with the impulses of her darker side. I always believed that if Ellie could just get through her thrill-seeking youth, she would emerge a more profound person born of experience and earned wisdom.

I gaze at the expanse of snow and ice across the river; I am just beginning to feel the warmth of the wood stove. The Wolf Creek house is where Ellie seemed most free and happy. Will the laughter of my other two children and my grandchildren ever again give life to this house?

The gulf between our human knowledge and our human spirit is a mystery that will not be solved by more information or technology. We have strayed from our connection to the earth—and despite the complexities of our scientific understanding—it becomes more difficult to explain birth, death, and tragedy. We no longer draw insights from watching nature. Most of us spend more time in front of a computer screen than in the natural environment for which we were designed. What now prepares us, emotionally and spiritually, for the inevitable experience of death that we share with all life forms?

Looking out onto the West Fork of the San Juan and experiencing the seasonal changes helps me become part of life's cycle, including Ellie's brief, but happy, twenty years. I watch the flowing river—always changing and giving life on its inevitable journey to the ocean's expanse.

I remember an old, swaybacked doe that protected her fawns in the willows each summer, year after year. Hoping to see her annual twins romping in the high grass this past summer, I watched and waited for her in vain. Where was she? I so wanted her appearance to refuel my hope. Still, there were the chubby bluebirds, lined along the fence, watching me as I fixed the gate.

Nature's lessons start with birth and new life. How does all this ease the ache of Ellie's passing? Does turning this over to what is simply unknowable replace a time of questioning with one of acceptance? How will I assimilate this loss? I don't even *want* to get completely beyond the loss. When asked how many children I have, I still say three. So much of Ellie is with me in dreams and memories and daily moments. Is she in heaven? Is her spirit as close as my shadow?

Today. I am a doctor trained in anesthesiology and pain management with firsthand experience of the one pain we least understand. My own journey of healing from heartache intersects with my vocation of helping others heal from pain. The resulting collision of personal and professional challenges has set off an array of questions for me.

Many of these questions are the same ones that agonize every heartache sufferer. How will I ever survive this? Why does it hurt so much in my chest? Why do people keep saying I will "get over" this? Will time alone help me get through it? How am I to understand what I am experiencing?

Other questions surface from my life as a physician. Why haven't we identified this pain in our review of symptoms? How can we talk about it in a way that is compassionate as well as practical? How can I watch and listen for signs of acute heartache among my patients? How can I help educate my healthcare colleagues about the risks of, and treatments for, heartache? What have we learned from heartbreak syndrome?

This book has been my way of pursuing those questions. After years of pondering the answers, I realized that the best way for me to understand heartache was to put the emotional and medical dimensions side by side. We may never resolve the deepest mysteries of heartache, but we can learn strategies to take action as opposed to helpless suffering. Looking at both sides of this universal human condition has been like focusing both barrels of a pair of binoculars. The medical and emotional questions posed in this book challenge us to look simultaneously through two different lenses in the hope of seeing the integrated image with more clarity. In doing so, we can begin to treat the whole person.

2

IF HEARTACHE IS EMOTIONAL, WHY DOES IT FEEL SO PHYSICAL?

The physical pain of grief has become, with time, a permanent
wound in the soul, a sorrow that will last as long as the body does.
—Andre Dubus[2]

One father wrote this upon learning of the death of his son in
a motor vehicle accident:

> It's as though all the air has been sucked out of the
> room, and you can barely breathe. There's such a
> sense of disbelief. Time stands still, and your mind
> refuses to accept the news as reality. And then—as
> the truth of it begins to take hold—you feel like
> you want to die yourself. I wanted to die so that the
> pain would stop.[3]

2   Andre Dubus, *Broken Vessels* (Boston: David R. Godine, 1992), p. 138.
3   Greg Laurie, *Hope for Hurting Hearts* (City: publisher, 2008), p. 40.

We think of heartache as emotional, but it actually feels very physical. Here is how another person described it:

With the kids gone, I had a miserable day. It bothered me all day and it wasn't until late that I realized what I was feeling.

It was heartache.

...As I got into the truck, I had that overwhelming sadness and hollowness in my chest, an aching throughout my entire body. It was as if a piece of me were missing. Like, somehow, a section of my chest had been removed. It was just outside me, but I couldn't grab it, nor get it back. And I wanted it back. I wanted *them* back. At that moment I thought; "I would do *anything* to be near them again." That's when I recognized Heartache as my companion.[4]

Devastating news or the realization of loss can trigger a range of symptoms:

- Pain in the arm
- Tightness in the throat
- Heaviness in the chest
- Breathlessness
- Chest pain
- Dizziness
- Profuse sweating
- Nausea

Have you noticed that many of these same symptoms accompany a heart attack? Heartache certainly makes us feel as if the heart is under attack. Thanks to research on so-called "Broken Heart Syndrome," we now know that

---

4   Jon Bohn, "Thru the Looking Glass into MS and Cancer," http://www.lookingglass.mi.org/ttl_archive/2004_12.html, downloaded September 19, 2009.

heartache precipitates major changes in the heart and vascular system. Emotional trauma can produce the same symptoms as a heart attack. The emotional impact triggers a cascade of physiological events, just as an abrupt chemical change adversely affects heart function.

Heartache doesn't just feel physical; it *is* physical. It is an actual bodily event. Technically speaking, it is an abrupt chemical change that has a negative effect on heart function. The heart is not only an organ: it is also the essence of a person. The human body cannot be reduced to a simple metabolic machine. Conversely, we spiritualize away the heart's physical reality when we describe heartache as merely an emotional condition. We set up a false division when we attempt to distinguish between the physical and the metaphorical heart.

The heart is both a physical reality and a spiritual mystery.

Researchers at Johns Hopkins University School of Medicine have named "broken heart syndrome" for patients who experienced sudden emotional stress and then developed symptoms suggesting an acute heart attack.[5] These were not people who were already suffering from heart disease. Researchers have concluded, "exaggerated sympathetic stimulation"—such as the fight or flight response to stress—"is probably central to the cause of this syndrome."

There are two other phrases commonly used to describe this phenomenon, both of which are related to the balloon-like shape of the left ventricle when the heart is under this kind of stress: "apical ballooning syndrome (ABS)" and "takotsubo cardiomyopathy" (named by Japanese physicians in the early

---

5   Ilan S. Wittstein, MD, et al., "Neurohumoral Features of Myocardial Stunning Due to Sudden Emotional Stress," *The New England Journal of Medicine* (10 Feb. 2005), vol. 352, no. 6, 539-548.

1990s for the balloon-shaped pot used by Japanese fishermen to catch octopuses).[6]

In extreme cases this phenomenon can be fatal, but in most cases immediate and even long-term physical changes result. Are these physical changes dangerous? It depends on one's health. Some people are more fragile and therefore susceptible to subtle changes in the heart. Others will find their activity level and energy affected or reduced—potentially dangerous consequences.

I got a phone call from a friend whose eighty-five-year-old mother had just been admitted to the hospital with deep, aching chest pain, and shortness of breath. Her skin was clammy, and all of her muscles ached.

Five days earlier, the youngest son of the elderly mother had been in a motorcycle accident. He had already been a source of chronic underlying heartache for her because of his substance abuse issues. Now, as she had feared, his behavior had led him to serious injury. Emotionally devastated, she had kept watch on him around the clock in the ICU, trying to comfort him as he lay inert in a hospital bed with head wounds and multiple fractures throughout his body. He was not expected to live.

My friend now had two hospitalized family members! Doctors performed tests on her mother.[7] They showed no

---

6   For a summary of the Japanese literature, see G. William Dec, MD, "Recognition of the Apical Ballooning Syndrome in the United States," *American Heart Association Journal* (Circulation 2005) 111:388-390, posted online at http://circ.**ahajournals.org**/cgi/content/full/circulationaha;111/4/388. See also AA Elesber, "Four-Year Recurrence Rate and Prognosis of the Apical Ballooning Syndrome," *Journal of the American College of Cardiology* (July 2007), vol. 50, no. 5:448-452.

7   Tests included an EKG (a rhythm study of the electrical activity of the heart), an echocardiogram (the use of sound waves to create a moving picture of the heart), a coronary angiography (a dye study of the vessels feeding the heart), and blood tests to reveal troponins, markers indicating heart injury.

damage to the heart muscle or to the vessels feeding the heart. Blood levels of chemicals released from an injured heart were negative. However, her echocardiogram showed a marked decrease in the contraction of her left ventricle, which pumps blood out of the heart back into the body, and in her ejection fraction (the percentage of blood pumped from the left ventricle to the body with each contraction). Clearly, she had not experienced a heart attack, but her heart function had been seriously compromised. Left untreated, this loss of function could have deteriorated into life-threatening congestive heart failure or a heart attack.

The cardiologist told the family that their mother was experiencing broken heart syndrome. Her emotional crisis had precipitated her physical crisis. With careful monitoring and medical care in the hospital, supported by emotional nurturing from family and friends, she had a good chance to survive without heart damage.

Most people recover from this kind of stress cardiomyopathy, but in a susceptible few it can cause heart damage or even sudden death. Had this elderly woman's heartache not been diagnosed and properly treated as an acute life-threatening process requiring treatment by her physician, my friend could well have had two family members lingering on the edge of death.

We can be grateful that research has narrowed the gap between emotional pain and evidence-based medicine. Today, both the general public as well as the professional medical community can enlarge their understanding of heartache and take proactive measures in response to personal crisis.

The physical symptoms of grief were documented in Eric Lindemann's groundbreaking study of those affected by a fire at the Coconut Grove nightclub in Boston after a football game between Harvard and Yale in 1942. Lindemann studied the acute and delayed reaction of family members of the 492 victims, noting that they described their pain as "sensations of somatic distress occurring in waves lasting from twenty minutes to an hour at a time, a feeling of tightness in the throat, choking with shortness of breath, need for sighing, and an empty feeling in the abdomen, lack of muscular power, and an intense subjective distress described as tension or mental pain."[8]

However, until the advent of "broken heart syndrome" as a medical concept we had no scientific documentation of heart pain associated with heartache. Now we can substantiate the intuitive knowledge of thousands of years. Heartache is not only a crushing emotional experience: it is an injury to the body. Dr. Stephen T. Sinatra, a cardiologist turned psychotherapist, comments that medical science is beginning to pay closer attention to the connections between the brain and the heart. "Today, some cardiologists speak not only of angina, arrhythmia or heart attack, but also of heartache: the result of the loss of vital relationships. This heartache can eventually lead to heartbreak, or the literal breaking down of heart function."[9]

As an anesthesiologist for an open-heart surgical team, I was trained to keep the heart muscle as viably balanced

---

8   E. Lindemann, "Symptomatology and management of acute grief," *American Journal of Psychiatry* 101 (1944):141.

9   Stephen T. Sinatra, MD, *Heartbreak and Heart Disease: A Mind / Body Prescription for Healing the Heart* (New Canaan, CT: Keats Publishing, 1999), 43.

as possible while the surgeons operated. It was a very concrete, technical, left-brained relationship. Because of my life circumstances, I have been forced into an expanded relationship with the heart. In the past I treated the heart as an organ to be kept alive. My new lens has revealed it to be the seat of emotional trauma as well. Now the challenge is to close the gap between the hard science of evidence-based medicine, which treats the heart as muscle, and the soft science of intuitive wisdom, which treats the heart as metaphor.

3

WHAT IS ACTUALLY HAPPENING IN MY HEART WHEN I AM EXPERIENCING HEARTACHE?

Grief is physically demanding.
—Alan D. Wolfelt[10]

Late nights in the intensive care unit (ICU) of a hospital are filled with constant sounds: a discordant, orchestral ensemble of varying heart beat monitors, the puff-pounding of ventilators, and the occasional cries and sighs of patients and their relatives. In its own disjointed patterns, this mixture of sounds signals the earnest attempts to continue the rhythm of life.

In this setting one late July night, I was called to evaluate the dwindling life forces of a twenty-nine-year-old man with a severe head injury and trauma to multiple body parts from a motorcycle accident. The heart monitor and electroencephalograph (EEG) monitoring his brain activity

---

10   Alan D. Wolfelt, PhD, *Healing a Friend's Grieving Heart: 100 Practical Ideas for Helping Someone You Love through Loss* (Fort Collins, CO: Companion Press, 2001), #19.

indicated that he was brain dead, and he had an irregular, slowing heart wave pattern.

I needed to discuss the truth of his imminent death with his young wife. I found her pacing the lounge outside the ICU surrounded by five children, ages one through eight. When I told her the devastating news with as much compassion as possible, she clutched her hand to her chest over her heart.

"Doctor, any minute now my heart is going to burst!" she exclaimed. In desperation, she pointed to her five children.

"Look at them," she said. "If I die too, they're all going to be orphans. You have to help me!"

I tried to calm her, but she could not catch her breath. She said the room was turning gray. She was profoundly emotionally distraught, and she felt the heavy pressure on her heart was unbearable. She perceived that her life force was diminishing along with that of her husband.

This event occurred several years ago, before the availability of medical documentation detailing the physiological consequences of the "Broken Heart Syndrome." Now we know that an intricate, complex pattern of physical events occurs in the heart itself. For the purposes of discussion, we can reduce this pattern to two of its primary phenomena.

First, when people say they are in "shock" or clutch their heart upon receiving sudden bad news, they are feeling the consequences of a huge increase in *catecholamines,* naturally occurring substances in the body released during times of sudden stress. This is exactly what is happening when we experience a rush of adrenaline.

Heartache can have a massive effect on the release of catecholamines, increasing their level in the blood as much as thirty-four times their normal level. This is more than double the estimated level of a person experiencing an acute heart attack! This extraordinary level of catecholamines radically changes the balance of blood flow to the vessels of the heart and other major organs of the body.

When catecholamines flood the system like this, they may cause spasms of the coronary arteries as well as a toxic effect on the heart muscle itself.[11]

In addition to the release of catecholamines, the second major shock effect sustained by the heart is in its *ejection fraction,* the percentage of blood pumped out of the left ventricle (the big chamber of the heart) with each heartbeat. This blood carries nutrients and oxygenated blood to the body. In a normal ejection fraction, approximately 55 percent of the blood in the left ventricle is pumped to the body with each beat of the heart. Under acute emotional distress, the ejection fraction can fall to only 15 percent—significantly reducing the oxygenated blood available to the body tissues. This means the body isn't getting the nutrients it needs for its organs, including the heart, to function properly.

An article in the February 2005 *New England Journal of Medicine* stated that heartache can cause a thirty-four-fold increase in catecholamine release like epinephrine [adrenaline] and norephineprine [noradrenaline].[12] In contrast, acute heart attack can cause only a four-fold increase in catecholamine release. Some typical effects of a catecholamine surge are increase in heart rate, blood pressure, and blood glucose levels and a general reaction of the sympathetic nervous stimulation (see figure 3.1).

---

11   Press release dated February 9, 2005, Johns Hopkins Medicine, http://www.hopkinsmedicine.org/Press_releases/2005/02_10_05.html
12   Ilan S. Wittstein, MD, et al., "Neurohumoral Features of Myocardial Stunning Due to Sudden Emotional Stress," *The New England Journal of Medicine* (10 Feb. 2005), vol. 352, no. 6, 539-548.

Catecholamine	Natural catecholamine actions [as a neurotransmitter]
Epinephrine [adrenaline]	Increased vascular resistance by constriction of blood vessels to the skin and body organs.
	Increased contraction of the heart.
	Increased heart rate.
	Increased oxygen requirements of the heart.
Norepinephrine [noradrenaline]	Peripheral vasoconstriction [as opposed to central constriction of the heart]
	Increased contraction of the heart.
	Increased oxygen consumption of the heart.
	Dilation of the arteries of the heart, in some cases.
Dopamine: precursor to norepinephrine	Variable reactions depending on the level: low, medium, high. Example: Low levels of dopamine can cause high blood flow to the kidneys; high levels of dopamine can reduce blood flow to the kidneys.

FIGURE 3.1. Specific actions of the three major catecholamines.[13]

---

13   For recent research on the role of catecholamine excess in broken heart syndrome, see R. Todd Hurst, MD, et al., "Takotsubo Cardiomyopathy: A Unique Cardiomyopathy with Variable Ventricular Morphology," *Journal of the American College of Cardiology: Cardiovascular Imaging* (June 2010), vol. 6 no. 3, 641-649.

This young wife and mother had evidently been experiencing a catecholamine surge resulting in increased blood pressure, increased heart rate, and decreased blood flow to the heart. At that moment, her heart was asked to pump harder—but with diminished oxygen supply. Each heart muscle cell received less oxygen (a condition known as *ischemia*) with resultant chest pressure and pain. But for her youth, her children may well have become orphans.

Inaccurately, I assumed at the time that her response to the imminent loss of her husband was fundamentally emotional rather than physical. Now, I would treat her as a patient as well and possibly admit her to the hospital for observation, sedation, and medical support for her cardiac function.[14] I would call the social worker or pastoral chaplain to organize support from family and friends. Further, I might order acute observation to monitor her every heartbeat.

Her follow-up care would be organized to include possible treatments such as:

- Ongoing monitoring of her heart
- Appropriate, temporary medications
- Psychological support
- Prayer, relaxation techniques, or meditation
- Monitored physical activity

---

14   For recent research on diagnosing broken heart syndrome, see Mohammed Reza Movahed, "Important Echocardiographic Features of Takotsubo or Stress-Induced Cardiomyopathy that Can Aid Early Diagnosis," *Journal of the American College of Cardiology: Cardiovascular Imaging* (November 2010), vol. 3 no. 11, 1200-1201.

This care would promote the timely correction of the dangerous cardiac manifestations of acute heartache and initiate longer-term help for her path to recovery.

If you are worried that a family member might be experiencing acute physical symptoms of heartache, you can reassure him or her that a sudden stressor can feel very physical in the middle of a severe emotional crisis. It is key to remain present and to observe the sufferer during the early hours of shock. Watch for signs of physical distress: chest pain, difficulty breathing, and excessive anxiety. Most people need emotional support, but some need medical evaluation if the physical symptoms become increasingly intense.

Now that we know that physical events are occurring in the heart when we experience heartache, the next question is the consequences of these events upon the heart. Two primary scenarios of catecholamine surge are dangerous to the heart. Both of them can be life threatening.

In the first scenario, damage to the heart muscle may occur. The marked increase in catecholamines acts directly on the heart. For example, when there is reduced oxygen to the heart, epinephrine can attach onto receptor sites on the heart cells, asking the heart for more work than it can provide (and leading to congestive heart failure). The catecholamine surge causes an increase in blood pressure, an increase in heart rate, and stimulation of the heart to increase its force of contraction.

At this point a "Catch-22" ensnares the heart. The catecholamines make demands upon the heart that require increased oxygen consumption. At the same time, the catecholamines are restricting the oxygen supply to the heart. They contract the coronary artery vessels, so that instead of being big and open the vessels become small and narrow, "pinching" off the delivery of vital nutrients to the heart. This starves the heart of what it needs to restore health and wholeness.

Essentially, in this scenario the heart is asked to perform more vigorously with less of what it needs for that performance. This ischemia (decreased oxygen to the tissue of the heart) most often produces pain. The pain may be felt in the chest or referred to the shoulder, arms, jaw, or upper abdomen. Some people experience a profound pressure as if a great weight had just been placed upon their chest. If the heart muscle ischemia is diagnosed and treated rapidly, the heart muscle can be saved. If a significant amount of the heart muscle is damaged, the patient may die or have a chronically weakened heart muscle, as occurs in congestive heart failure.

In the second possible scenario, disruption of the heart's rhythms may occur. When the increase in catecholamines starves the heart muscle cells of oxygen and nutrients, the risk of irregular heart rhythms increases. Ventricular fibrillation is a severely abnormal heart rhythm, or *arrhythmia,* that causes death unless immediately treated. The ventricles, the two large chambers of the heart, pump blood to the body. When they are fibrillating, instead of maintaining a regular, productive beat, they quiver like a sack of worms— pitching the heart into a chaotic rhythm without organized contraction. The result is ineffective heart contraction. When body tissues do not get enough blood, within minutes the body experiences damage to or destruction of its major organs. First and foremost, the brain is harmed, and secondly, the heart.

If you have ever seen a heart monitor, you know what a rhythm strip looks like—that zigzagging line on a screen or paper printout showing the rhythm of the heart. You see regular, recurring waveforms with normal heart function. Ventricular fibrillation causes an erratic variation in the shape and amplitude of the waveform, as if a palsied hand were scribbling them up and down.

The cascade of acute heartache, the increase in catecholamines, the rapid change in heart function, and the possible development of arrhythmias, heart failure, and death emphasize the need for patients and doctors alike to raise a red flag when appropriate. Look and listen to heartache sufferers carefully and act immediately to avoid or retard the heartache cascade.

Intervention in such cases is possible by decreasing *the patient interval,* the time it takes the patient to get medical help. Why should you see a doctor if you are feeling symptoms of heartache? First, you must avoid a fatal arrhythmia such as ventricular fibrillation. This is especially true for those with preexisting heart disease such as coronary artery disease, which is a hardening of the arteries of the blood vessels of the heart. Put acute heartache on top of that condition, and you will be vulnerable for a heart attack or a fatal arrhythmia.

The leading cause of death in the United States and Canada is sudden cardiac arrest. Immediate intervention can be taken with a defibrillator, which snaps the heart back into a regular rhythm. This is why defibrillators are often deployed like fire extinguishers in public places such as commercial aircraft. The Center for Disease Control and Prevention estimates that

330,000 people die annually in out-of-hospital or emergency room settings from coronary heart disease and associated irregular heart rhythms.

The second reason to see a doctor promptly if you are feeling acute heartache is to re-establish blood flow to your heart, sparing the muscle from possible irreversible damage. This is much like getting water to a plant that has wilted. If you get there in time, you can restore the life of the plant. If you get there too late, the plant is starved of what it needs to survive, and it withers and dies.

For thousands of years we have intuitively known that a broken heart has physical consequences. "A dream deferred makes the heart grow sick," says the writer of Proverbs. But until recently, when it became so clearly delineated, we often explained away the physical consequences as something happening only in the brain.

For example, nearly a decade ago science writer Carl Zimmer commented upon "the strange concept of heartache":

> It may be metaphorical now, but originally it was supposed to be a purely physical description. From ancient Greece to the Renaissance, a strong tradition held that the heart contained a soul of its own that could perceive the outside world and produce feelings. Great thinkers from Aristotle to Thomas Hobbes were convinced that nerves delivered their signals to the heart rather than the brain. With the birth of neurology in the 1600s, the brain came to take a central place in the body as the

site of emotions and perceptions. Meanwhile, the heart was de-souled, transformed into a mechanical pump. But the tradition of the heart lives on, and not just in words like heartache. . . .

Thanks to catecholamine surges and ejection fractions, we now know that the ache is literally in the heart. Perhaps we have come full circle. It is no longer enough to speak of the heart as a soulless pump. How ironic that the medical reality of heartache might be the very occasion for restoring a more soulful understanding of the heart.

4

How Does Emotional Trauma Travel From the Head to the Heart?

Pain is no invading enemy, but a loyal messenger
dispatched by my own body to alert me to some danger.
—Paul Brand[15]

If you have ever been on the receiving end of words you never wanted to hear...

- "I'm sorry to say there's been an accident."
- "I'm afraid there were complications in the surgery."
- "I'm leaving you."
- "The test results came back positive."

...then you are familiar with the devastating thought that clutches at your heart, "How am I going to survive this? It'll kill me."

---

15   Quoted in Philip Yancey and Dr. Paul Brand, *Pain: The Gift Nobody Wants* (Grand Rapids: Zondervan, 1993), p. 80.

News like this is a virtual slam to the head. The brain receives stunning information, but how does this information simultaneously affect the heart?[16]

There are specific pathways that transmit this information at lightning speed from the brain to the heart. This information is sent from the brain by nerve pathways to an area in the spinal cord called the dorsal horn (which extends up and down the cord). The dorsal horn contains chemicals that transmit and modify signals along pathways to and from the brain as well as receptors—specialized areas that transfer information.

We will explore those pathways in a moment, but first we want to recognize why such technical information is important. It leads us to the concept of *plasticity.*

Brain researchers have discovered that the brain and the central nervous system have the remarkable ability to change the way they operate. This *plasticity* means that not only is the body hardwired to receive and recover from injury, but it can also change its own software, as it were, for dictating *how* it receives and recovers from injury. This built-in power to move toward harm or healing gives us the power to choose either self-destructive behavior or healing behavior.

In recent years, research has uncovered the good news that plasticity extends to the functions of the spinal cord, the major pathway from the brain out to the rest of the body (through the peripheral nervous system). Specifically, this pathway is the *dorsal horn* of the spinal cord (see diagram of spinal cord in cross section, below) where influences from mind and body converge to affect the balance of life.

---

16   For the potentially adverse effects of the brain upon the heart triggered by emotional or physiologic stress, see Eugene A. Hessel II, MD, FACS, "The Brain and the Heart," *Anesthesia and Analgesia* (Sept. 2006), vol. 103, no. 3:522-526.

Does it matter if you know a dorsal horn exists inside your spinal cord? Yes—emotional trauma travels from your brain to your heart via your dorsal horn! This knowledge gives you power to change how your body receives and responds to heartbreaking news.

The dorsal horn of the spinal cord is a primary pathway for the transmission of pain messages. The messages travel two ways: bottom-up, from the pain sites to the brain, and top-down, from the brain back out to the pain sites. This two-way "street" explains why biofeedback works in modifying pain: we can reprogram the brain to send out soothing messages to the pain sites instead of only sending pain alarms to the brain.

The dorsal horn itself is a kind of chemical soup, made up of ingredients such as epinephrine (adrenaline), norepinephrine, and serotonin. Although we don't yet understand exactly how this chemical soup operates in all respects, we do know its primary ingredients. We also know that the balance of ingredients affects the way we perceive physical pain and emotional stress. The composition of the chemical soup can change instantaneously, profoundly affecting the organs of the body such as by increasing or decreasing the blood flow to the heart.

Foremost among the ingredients of the dorsal horn's chemical soup are *neurotransmitters,* the chemicals that carry and modify signals along pathways to the brain by transmitting information between nerve cells; and *receptors,* specialized nerve cells (neurons) or parts of that nerve cell that transfer sensory information.

When a traumatic event happens, it triggers a barrage of painful impulses. Repetitive incoming signals increase the intensity and frequency of the pain message in the "wind-up phenomenon," sometimes leading to an imprint on the brain. This is the process of central sensitization. The nervous system retains physiological memory of the damage it has sustained, even if the pain impulse has been withdrawn.

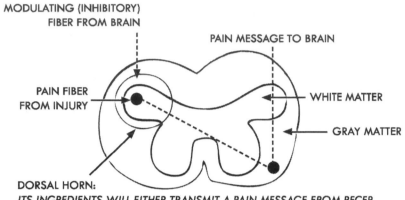

MODULATING (INHIBITORY) FIBER FROM BRAIN

PAIN MESSAGE TO BRAIN

PAIN FIBER FROM INJURY

WHITE MATTER

GRAY MATTER

DORSAL HORN:
ITS INGREDIENTS WILL EITHER TRANSMIT A PAIN MESSAGE FROM RECEP-TOR SITES TO THE BRAIN, INHIBIT THE PAIN MESSAGE AS THE BRAIN MODIFIES THE INCOMING PAIN SIGNALS, OR MAINTAIN AN IMPRINT OF A PAIN MESSAGE IN THE CENTRAL SENSITIZATION PHENOMENON.

FIGURE 4.1. Spinal cord, shown in cross-section.

Thanks to plasticity, the chemical balance within the dorsal horn can be changed by top-down stimuli, such as sudden bad news traveling from the brain out to the body, or by bottom-up stimuli, such as a pain message traveling from a hand on a hot stove back up to the brain.

In the "acute" phase of heartache, for example when we hear the news we've been dreading, the brain communicates to the heart through the chemical soup of the dorsal horn. Think of that region as a railroad station, and the neurotransmitters (catecholamines such as adrenaline) as the railroad cars. Picture the brain screaming at the dorsal horn, "Send out more cars! Send out more cars!" The entire body immediately feels the sudden sense of impending doom as the brain "slam" speeds along neurologic pathways through the spinal cord and its neurotransmitters out to organs of the body. The railroad station now changes the number of cars in the roundhouse and the number of cars sent out to organs of the body.

Remember that catecholamines can increase up to thirty-four times their normal presence? Now imagine these neurotransmitters—the "cars" sent out from the roundhouse—locking onto receptor sites in the heart. They have a profound effect on the heart, demanding that it beat harder and faster but paradoxically requiring it to do so without as much oxygen by restricting blood flow at the same time. Blood pressure is rising as well. Now the dynamics of the heart have been dramatically changed in a resulting condition known as *stress cardiomyopathy*.

However, this pathway for bad news reminds us of the presence of a pathway for healing. Thanks to the plasticity of the central nervous system, when heartache crushes us we can send top-down messages from the brain to the dorsal horn in order to stop the flood of cars leaving the railroad station. We can do this by learning to modify the negative physiologic effects of bad news. In the chemical soup of neurotransmitters at the dorsal horn, profound changes in the balance of chemicals can be made by prayer, meditation, biofeedback relaxation, and by turning fear and anxiety over to a greater source. We may need to seek help promptly to facilitate these interventions, which can increase blood flow to the coronary arteries and decrease the oxygen consumption of the heart muscle. They can also lower elevated blood pressure.

An excellent reference on the effects of prayer and meditation on stress-induced states such as heartache is Dr. Herbert Benson's *Timeless Healing*. Benson coined the phrase "remembered wellness" to describe the placebo effect—a patient's belief in the possibility of healing based upon the body's memory of what it is like to be well.[17] He also developed the "relaxation response," the opposite of the body's flight-or-fight mechanism, as an aid to visualizing wellness, citing its potential to lower blood pressure, heart rate, breathing rate, and anxiety through activities such as meditative prayer (for example, the repetition of a focus such as "The Lord is my shepherd" with a passive disregard of intruding thoughts), progressive muscular relaxation, jogging, swimming, or yoga.[18]

Knowing how emotional trauma travels from the head to the heart provides a sense of mastery, and even hope, because we know we can exercise our power to offset the adverse physical effects of heartbreaking news.

---

17   Herbert Benson, MD, *Timeless Healing: The Power and Biology of Belief* (New York: Scribner, 1997), p. 20.
18   Benson, *Timeless Healing,* p. 134.

5

WHY HAS THE MEDICAL COMMUNITY BEEN SLOW TO ADDRESS THE PHYSICAL SYMPTOMS OF HEARTACHE?

The reductive, mechanistic view of the body grants no privilege to the "integrated whole." Modern medical science has evolved for most of [the twentieth] century as if the mind played no part in disease... even now, the mind is seen mostly as a kind of nuisance that can cause a placebo effect that has to be factored out of studies before the "real" impact of a drug or surgical technique can be determined.
—Chip Brown[19]

Twenty-five years ago, at the peak of my anesthesiology career, I had another chance to redefine my relationship with the heart. Married with three small children, I was a distance runner who exercised to relieve the stresses of a demanding practice. I learned I had an enlarged heart because of a mitral valve defect.

---

19   Chip Brown, *Afterwards,You're a Genius: Faith, Medicine, and the Metaphysics of Healing* (New York: Riverhead/Penguin Putnam, 1998), p. 47.

I could choose to live with a long, slow decline in function as my heart stretched until it could no longer pump blood through my body; or I could opt for a temporary fix by a mechanical valve replacement, which would forestall the decreased heart function for a few more years yet require a future of repeated heart surgeries. Following the mechanical valve replacement surgery, I would also be placed on the anticoagulant drug Coumadin, which would decrease my chances of an active life while increasing the risks of stroke and other complications. I faced a severely limited lifestyle very different from the one I had known.

This was a stress-producing quandary. Therefore, I concentrated on spiritual practices that would help me with the emotional turmoil I was experiencing in my preparation to make this choice. Early morning meditations helped offset the feeling that I was in a black tunnel with no guarantee that I would ever find my way out into the light of a healthy future with my loved ones.

My heart-sickness gave me a healthy respect for the complexities of treating the heart. I sensed that the problem with my physical heart was connected to deeper issues within my soul, and that my journey of physical healing was also a process of inward purification. A pastor friend and I began the practice of bathing everything in prayer—including my prognosis. We spent time listening and asking for guidance. His intuition was that we should not be limited by the conventions of Western medicine. Together, we developed a sense of peace in anticipation of a therapeutic alternative to the surgical answer. He wisely suggested that I study the problem at the university medical school library nearby. My experience as the anesthesiologist for an open-heart team would at least give me a place to begin.

I began to experience the quiet calm and confidence that so uniquely arises from prayer. As I continually turned over my fears and uncertainties, I found that creative ideas flowed. I discovered information quickly, as if I were being guided to just the right references. Answers that were difficult to obtain on my own came to me easily. I believe that authentic spiritual practice of any tradition, far from shutting down the intellectual dimension as some suppose, actually enhances cognitive thinking—and that was my experience.

My research led me to the so-called "French Correction" procedure developed by a world-famous surgeon who had been performing heart-valve *repairs* in France. He would later teach his repair method to doctors in the United States. His highly artistic method of repairing the valve rendered replacement unnecessary. I chose to travel across the Atlantic in order to have this innovative, yet risky and experimental, surgery. The operation would occur in a hospital with developing-world conditions, where patients and caregivers of all nationalities, cultures, and languages shared hospital wards and used body language to communicate with each other.

In the days leading up to my departure for the operation, I prepared mentally and emotionally by meditating each day in the early morning. I followed an active breathing process recommended in Richard Foster's classic book, *Celebration of Discipline*. Afterwards I would visualize heart and soul leaving my body and slowly rising up into the dark, early-morning sky of Santa Fe, drifting through the changing colors of the clouds into the healing presence of God. Through these interludes, I came to believe that my heart was already in the process of being healed.

The night before I left for Paris, Native American friends visited me from the nearby San Ildefonso Pueblo. Dora Tse-Pe and her family arrived in their pickup truck to present a gift: one of Dora's beautiful black-on-black pots that she had made from the earth of her ancestral lands. It was a symbolic and spiritual gift to the French surgeon halfway across the globe. My surgery was scheduled very close to the San Ildefonso feast day, and I knew that Dora's clan would be offering prayers, dancing, and conducting religious ceremonies for me. This spirit-filled medicine was a powerful comfort to me—and perhaps to the surgeon as well—for the operation proved successful.

It took my conversion from doctor to patient to help me understand that treating the heart involves mystery as well as mechanics. This experience took me well beyond the traditionally Western solutions of pills and shots and surgeries. It so profoundly affected me that I changed medical specialties as a result. This awakening took me deeper into my own Christian beliefs and planted in me the desire to search for and share the relationships of the mind, body, and spirit dimensions of pain. When I later experienced the enduring heartache of losing my daughter Ellie, I became more specifically interested in the intertwining of the physiological, emotional, and spiritual aspects of heartache.[20]

In my experience both as an anesthesiologist and as a pain doctor, I can testify that heartache is one of the most neglected and misunderstood categories of pain. When news

---

20   For prescriptive advice on addressing the spiritual and physical dimensions of heartache simultaneously, see chapter 7 of this book, "How Can I Learn to Treat My Own Heartache?" (pp. 53–64).

of broken heart syndrome spread through the media, it raised awareness about the physical dangers of heartache. [21]

Many people are familiar with the scenario we experienced recently at our pain center: a couple in their eighties were frequent visitors for treatment of the wife's spinal stenosis (a narrowing of the spinal canal). One injection would give her nine months of increased activity and decreased pain. On a certain day when she was scheduled for her next injection, her husband showed up alone and in some distress. He reported to us that his wife was in the cardiac care unit. Through their daughter, we learned that she had died within a few days. Two weeks later, the daughter showed up at our clinic to let us know that her father had died as well. Apparently a cardiac event ended his life.

Such stories may be familiar, but the medical phenomenon of heartache is not. Western doctors conduct histories and physicals as the groundwork for diagnosing and treating patients. This is where the doctor-patient relationship starts. Every medical school teaches a format for taking a patient history and performing an initial physical examination. Heartache is not included in that format. Questions are not asked about heartache, grieving, and loss when taking the patient history. Therefore, heartache is not part of the differential diagnosis, and because it is not recognized, it is simply not considered in treatment.

When cardiologist Stephen Sinatra embarked upon a second career in psychoanalysis, he has written that his "real

---

21   For example, a 9 February 2005 press release from Johns Hopkins Medicine was picked up in a 9 February 2005 article in *USA Today* and a 10 February 2005 article in the *Washington Post*. Many news outlets picked up and ran the Associated Press article, "Docs: Heartbreak More than a Metaphor," dated 11 February 2005. On 16 November 2006, the Mayo Clinic released a follow-up study. Broken heart syndrome hit the news again recently with a 26 January 2010 article in the *Wall Street Journal*.

growth in cardiac healing began."[22] He studied emotional and psychological as well as physical risk factors in the attempt to more clearly understand the mind-body connection in heart disease:

> The psychological risk factors can be just as lethal as the more accepted physical risk factors. Although the epidemiological relationship between physical risk factors and heart disease is important to consider, it is also essential to note that the major physical risk factors (cigarette smoking, increased cholesterol, hypertension) are found in less than half of those who succumb to coronary artery disease. Therefore other factors must be considered. It is my belief that hidden emotional risk factors are the missing link. I believe that heart health depends on paying attention to the profound physical effects that emotions have upon the body. Emotions express themselves as behaviors and as physiological reactions that can place one at risk for heart disease. These are the "hidden risk factors" in heart disease that many cardiologists fail to acknowledge.[23]

In Western medicine the goal is to locate the specific cause of a disease with laboratory tests, radiological studies, and the history and physical examination of the patient. The medical process of determining the cause of disease is didactic

---

22   Stephen T. Sinatra, MD, F.A.C.C., C.B.T., *Heartbreak and Heart Disease: A Mind/Body Prescription for Healing the Heart* (New Canaan, CT: Keats Publishing, 1999), p. 3.
23   Sinatra, *Heartbreak and Heart Disease,* pp. 118-19.

and concrete. As psychologist James Lynch observes, "A few hundred years ago 'grief' was openly recognized as a cause of death. Today, however, a broken heart would never be listed as a cause of death in any United States hospital. We have grown far too 'medically wise' to tolerate such an ill-defined diagnosis. Patients now die of atherosclerosis, ventricular fibrillation, or congestive heart failure brought on by age, damaged hearts and arteries, or poor eating habits."[24]

Medical professionals in the United States are trained in evidence-based medicine. Our technological society is based on fixing material things, and medical training seldom acknowledges the spiritual aspects of illness. Most doctors are uncomfortable with mystery, especially in the medical arena.

Yet heartache is bound up with the condition of the body. Often, it may trigger a physical illness. The pain generator may be the heart, but the target organ can be anything from the heart itself to the gastrointestinal tract, as in ulcerative colitis or peptic ulcer disease; the urinary tract, such as pelvic pain or interstitial cystitis; skeletal, such as low back pain; skin problems, such as an acne outbreak; or pulmonary, such as in asthma. People also experience some degree of heartache with an abrupt loss of body function intrinsically connected to disease.

To acknowledge heartache as part of the disease, we move immediately beyond the concrete to the mystical. Seeking the scientific data about an illness is not incompatible with exploring the mystery embedded in that patient's illness. This is a departure from a search for laboratory values and radiological images to the arena of the unknown and unquantifiable, a difficult place for those trained in evidence-based methodology.

---

24   James J. Lynch, *The Broken Heart: The Medical Consequences of Loneliness* (New York: Basic Books, 1977), p. 56.

Ancient societies, which are closer to the earth and more accepting of suffering, treat heartache as a physical and spiritual reality. They have derived healing rituals designed to reconnect the sufferer with intimate relationships and with the larger community while addressing physical symptoms.

Anthropologist Richard Katz has documented the community dances of the Kung, a former hunting and gathering society living in the Kalahari Desert of southern Africa. Central to their culture is an all-night healing dance, performed on a nearly weekly basis, in which healing energies are gathered and extended to the whole community. "Being at a dance makes our hearts happy," the Kung say.[25]

Among the very first people I met upon returning from a tour of duty in Vietnam was a Native American Indian family—grandmother, mother, and daughter. Thirty-seven years later, I received a desperate call from the granddaughter asking me to come to the hospital where her eighty-six-year-old grandmother was terminally ill. The grandmother was the famous American Indian ethno-artist Pablita Velarde. She lay dying in the Western hospital surrounded by many traditional Pueblo Indian family and friends. They wanted to take her back to her Indian village of origin—the home of her spirit—to make her passage from earthly life.

Seeing this old friend in the hospital with an agonal breathing pattern, on a whopping fourteen liters of oxygen, it was clear to me that the spirit and the body were separating. Yet the young doctor at the hospital was reluctant to let her people take her home. So he was poring over laboratory results and X-rays, balancing the infusion drip filled with medication to maintain and sustain life, trying to reverse the

25   Richard Katz, *Boiling energy: Community Healing Among the Kalahari Kung* (Cambridge: Harvard Univ. Press, 1982), p. 34.

inevitable. He was focused on the science of medicine to the exclusion of the mystery of life and death.

Does the spirit or soul—the essence of the individual—leave the body simultaneously with the moment of physical death? Societies close to the earth, who walk daily a spiritual path like my friends from the New Mexico San Ildefonso Pueblo, may have insight into this question. It is yet another mystery that will never be solved by scientific advances. Where life and death are concerned, it seems that "now we are seeing in a mirror dimly, but then we will see clearly."[26]

Many of us live today less burdened by discomfort because of advances in medicine. We do not have to bite a bullet while being restrained for a necessary surgery with little or no sedation. Until a hundred years ago, that was the harsh reality of nearly any surgical procedure, and it is still true for much of the world today. Grateful as we can be for medical advances, we also want our healthcare providers to have the humility to seek help from other sources outside strictly scientific parameters. For example, a patient's spiritual beliefs may be the fundamental strength of their human spirit. This means the physician must examine the metaphorical heart of the patient. In doing so, the doctor moves beyond the competent technician or brilliant diagnostician to the healer within.

Most physicians altruistically sought a medical degree because of a fundamental desire to serve as caregivers. Some remain well-educated caretakers, while others grow jaded by years of overwork, a litigious society, entitled patients, and overbearing medical healthcare bureaucracies. Businessmen with little or no caretaker instinct now run health delivery systems. For many doctors, their innate orientation toward

---

26   *The Life Application Bible,* rev. ed. (Wheaton, IL: Tyndale, 1989), p. 2019, 1 Cor 13:11).

healing is eclipsed by the multiple stresses of a complex practice ruled by technology and the dictates of the business of practicing medicine.

Recovering the healer within necessitates the celebration of mystery in the midst of our culture's esteem for monetary worth, intellectual prowess, technological expertise, and physical stamina. There must be a letting go of some of these societal gratifications to honor the intuitive heart of the healer. Mystery is not a state of temporary ignorance that will disappear with more scientific information, but a reality that is essentially beyond human understanding. In recognizing this reality, it becomes easier to grasp the intangibles associated with heartache while acknowledging its tangible manifestations.

Our society views heartache as an agonizing emotional pain, though without the physical legitimacy of other symptoms such as migraine headaches, abdominal pain, or joint pain from arthritis. Naming heartache as a potential condition that may have significant physical impact gives it medical validity.

Recognizing the physical repercussions of heartache helps patients understand and legitimize what is happening to them. Sometimes there is a sense of relief with this knowledge. It is the beginning of planning treatment and creating a pathway from resignation to recovery.

Physicians need encouragement to make heartache a formal part of the history they take from patients. They can ask questions such as "Are you experiencing heartache at the present time? If so, are there associated physical symptoms such as heaviness in the chest or profound fatigue, beyond the deep sadness that you feel?" This kind of inquiry can externalize what is otherwise a hidden pain.

The realm of heartache represents the greatest divergence between professional medicine and the non-professional world of self-care. Pain practice, one of the newest professional specialties, has yet to catch up with this holistic emphasis. It is still concerned primarily with technique and medication.

It is unfortunate that we tend to skirt the issue of heartache rather than confront it, because it has core potential for the greatest change as well as the greatest distress. Some realities are accessible less by observation and analysis than by creativity and intuition. This understanding requires humility in the face of mystery.

6

How Can Medical Professionals Best Learn to Treat Heartache?

Getting well requires that the physician and the patient share in the healing process as a team.
—Dr. Stephen Sinatra[27]

My specialty as a pain doctor is one of the most rapid growth areas in medicine. The demand for professional care in pain management is far longer than the three-month waiting list at our New Mexico Pain & Wellness Centers in Santa Fe and Albuquerque. The names on the list represent individuals from all walks of life—poor and rich; Anglo, Indian, and Hispanic; barely-employed to independently wealthy; young, old, parents, children, neighbors, friends; some folks smiling, some scowling, and some patients staring vacantly. Pain respects no one. It is a reality of being human— as basic as eating and sleeping (or not).

27 Stephen T. Sinatra, MD, F.A.C.C., C.B.T., *Heartbreak and Heart Disease*, p. 24.

I spend my days listening to, exploring with, treating for, and following up on patients enduring all kinds of pain. It can be chronic pain from a long-ago injury that has never completely healed; acute pain from a recent accident or medical emergency; recurring pain dashing waves of illness against an already weakened body; pain associated with whiplash, herpes viruses, peripheral neuropathies, cancer, AIDS, arthritis, diabetes…and on and on, in endless forms. There is no question "if" we will experience pain—just "when" and "what kind" and "why"—and most importantly for my patients: "how do I make the pain stop?"

Our patients show up at our Pain Center because they have nowhere else to turn. The surgeons have done their job. The prescribing physician has run through a list of drugs. The therapists have suggested healthier coping strategies. Friends are wondering if the pain has moved from the body into the head. Coworkers are tired of hearing about it. Loved ones are just tired.

Pain treatment for these sufferers always involves a complex array of factors, because the pain event seeps into multi-layered dimensions—physical, psychological, emotional, spiritual. A further complication is that the experience of pain itself is not a static reality, but a dynamic, ever-changing phenomenon. Changing and reducing pain patterns requires attention to the unique host of contributing factors in how each individual experiences pain.

Heartache involves a complex nexus of factors as well. We often ignore heartache as a category of pain because we don't know how to reconcile its varying ways of manifesting itself on physical, psychological, and spiritual levels. Heartache makes us feel broken, empty, alone, and lost. It is a very private and intimate injury, which is why we hide it—we fear exposure. We fear further injury to that tender place if we expose it by admitting the hurt.

Yet as James Lynch illuminates in his studies of the body's response to dialogue, our hearts are deeply and profoundly affected by interaction with other human beings:

> So vital to human health is the language of our hearts that—if ignored, unheard, or misunderstood—it can produce terrible physical suffering, even premature death. The language of our hearts cries out to be heard. It demands to be understood. And it must not be denied. Our hearts speak with an eloquence that poets have always, and truly, sensed. It is for us to learn to listen and to understand. [28]

Physicians will not be motivated to treat heartache as a legitimate medical condition until they become aware of the physiological consequences of untreated heartache.

Some patients believe that the doctor's office is not an appropriate context for revealing emotional trauma, but when it affects physical status it becomes an important factor in the physician's review. Often, simply by asking the question, "Are you experiencing a loss, grief, or heartache?" a doctor can bring emotional pain out into the open.

A cardiologist found himself examining a fellow physician, a sixty-four-year-old surgeon who was planning to retire

---

28   Lynch, *A Cry Unheard*, p. 10.

after a four-decade career. The surgeon's first priority had always been the education of his four children and continuing education for his wife and himself. Throughout his career, he had diligently and routinely placed some money in a retirement fund, finally accumulating enough to retire modestly with a reasonable sense of security for the future. Five years earlier, he'd had a heart attack and had undergone successful coronary artery bypass surgery.

Then the 2008 economic recession hit, and his assets lost 40 percent of their value. Anxiety over this loss of security hit hard. Experiencing acute chest pain and a feeling of impending doom, he notified his son, who took him to the emergency department of a nearby hospital. An entire cardiac evaluation was done, which showed a decrease in the ejection fraction and an increased catecholamine level, but a normal EKG, and normal blood cardiac enzymes. The blood vessels that feed the heart were also studied and found to be clearly open with little plaque formation. Aware of the reasons for anxiety and consequent pain, the cardiologist diagnosed broken heart syndrome.

The surgeon was hospitalized, observed in the Intensive Care Unit, sedated, and his blood pressure was managed. His son brought their rabbi to reassure family and friends and to encourage the patient about his future. This circle of supporters helped him view his financial situation with calm and confidence. He began walking the family dog twice a day and began spending more time outdoors. He joined an exercise program at the Cardiac Rehab Center, which he had been too busy to do after his heart attack five years previously. He met weekly with a group of men to study scriptures at the synagogue. He and his wife planned a trip to see the Southwest Indian culture. Focusing less on illness and financial fears and developing a more vital hope for the future, he essentially became actively involved in his own *well*ness.

Patients may need permission to express emotional issues, and the doctor's role must shift from treating illness to treating the whole person. Sometimes it is necessary to explore the whole in order to fully understand the parts; the doctor's office needs to be an arena for integrating emotional and physical health. This approach requires healthcare providers to practice what has traditionally been called "the art of medicine." Bernadine Healy, MD, sums it up in four principles:

- Mastery—to gain expertise, not just experience
- Humility—to connect with the entire human being, not just the disease or organ, and to listen actively to the patient in order to learn rather than defend
- Individuality—to pay attention to the uniqueness of each patient
- Morality—to respect the privacy and content of the doctor-patient relationship[29]

Practicing medicine is fundamentally a fine-tuning of the powers of observation. Every day, doctors practice reading body language: the unspoken information people reveal about themselves by their actions, looks, gestures, and dress. Does the patient appear depressed, anxious, guarded, fragile, distracted?

29   Bernadine Healy, MD, *US News &World Report* (15 July 2007), posted online at http:// health.usnews.com/usnews/health/articles/070715/23healy.htm, downloaded January 15, 2010.

If the patient appears to be grieving it would be important to assess where and how grief is affecting the patient physically. In her book *On Death and Dying,* Elisabeth Kübler-Ross has identified five classic stages of processing grief:

(1) Denial—"I feel fine."
(2) Anger—"Why me?" and "It's not fair."
(3) Bargaining—"I'll do anything to restore the past."
(4) Depression—"I'm so sad. Why bother with anything?"
(5) Acceptance—"It's going to be okay."[30]

Other grief experts, such as George A. Bonanno,[31] point out that individuals experience grief differently, and not everyone goes through the same sequence of stages. Bonanno emphasizes the human capacity to thrive after difficult events—a resilience that provides its own momentum toward recovery.

Patients often have a bodily knowledge about their physical and emotional status. They may be asking the doctor to validate their inner knowing rather than to marginalize it as "just" an emotional crisis. Patients live moment to moment in their bodies, and some are acutely aware of even subtle changes. Doctors need to listen actively with the objective to learn rather than to defend their preconceived medical opinions. Other patients remain in denial and need help facing the reality of heartache because of the potential adverse physical and emotional consequences.

---

30   Elisabeth Kübler-Ross, *On Death and Dying* (New York: Scribner, 1997), p. 12.

31   George A. Bonanno PhD, *The Other Side of Sadness: What the New Science of Bereavement Tells Us about Life after Loss* (New York: Basic Books, 2009).

Sometimes we underestimate the effects of grief and overlook its physical manifestations.

When our children were nine, seven, and two, we lived in the high desert countryside outside of Santa Fe, New Mexico. One day the children found a tiny baby raven at the bottom of a piñon tree. He was plump, unable to fly, and there were no parents in sight. They brought the baby bird home, and we all hand-fed it every two hours. We read in depth about ravens, learning about their exceptional intelligence, family reunions, and use of tools. We read accounts of how ravens in the Old Testament fed the prophet Elijah while he hid in a cave, how the Vikings took them into battle for good luck, and how Native Americans honored their intelligence and craftiness by naming leaders after them.

"Butch" the raven grew quickly, imprinting on our family and becoming an integral part of the family menagerie, which at the time included dogs, cats, chickens, and rabbits. When he was fully grown, Butch dominated all the animals, riding on the back of the golden retriever and sampling all the other animals' food bowls first. He was effervescent and bombastic, playing with the children by hiding trinkets and coaching them from the backboard of the basketball court. During long mountain-bike rides, Butch rode on my shoulder, occasionally flying off into the horizon and returning to a soft landing on the same shoulder. He had many voices and even mimicked a few words in English. He would greet visitors—who were by turns afraid and entertained—with multiple voices while perched comfortably on my shoulder. All were amazed at his gregarious presence, his tenderness, and his humor.

When a roving coyote killed Butch, heartache struck the entire family. Emily, age seven, would clutch her hand to her heart and express that it hurt there. Eric, age nine, was physically ill with nausea and vomiting and missed school for two days.

Even children experience physical manifestations of heartache: chest pain, vomiting, decreased energy, and depression. These symptoms represent some change in the flow dynamics to the heart and other organs and the increase of catecholamine, even in the very young. The cultural and social pressures that encumber adults do not restrain children from unguarded expressions of heartache. For any children who have congenital heart abnormalities or whose health is frail, there should be increased vigilance surrounding the incidence of heartache. Any physical manifestations of heartache in children must be taken as seriously as those of adults. Every year we hear of adolescents and young adults dying after extreme exertion on the athletic field due to exhaustion or heat stroke exacerbating an existing congenital condition. Heartache can function as a similar accelerator.

It's important for doctors to educate themselves on types of heartache, since heartache is not always a loss of relationship. Treatment options will vary depending upon the individual and the source of the heartache. For example, here is a doctor's list of how to recognize different types of heartache:

- *Acute heartache from a sudden tragic event, such as loss of a loved one or loss of a beloved pet, or from a violent trauma of some kind.* The development of a life-threatening physical condition is higher for people with pre-existing conditions such as coronary artery disease, congestive heart failure, high blood pressure, severe anxiety, and depression (a chronic debilitating disease). Chronic pain is most likely going to increase from any added heartache.

- *Chronic heartache*—whether passive, such as in years of unresolved grief—or repressed, such as in displaced response to heartache.
- *Loss of body function*—for example, loss of a limb—and consequent loss of self-image, loss of work capability, and a sensed loss of wholeness.
- *Loss of relationship*—any intimate connection that has been severed in any way.
- *Loss of hope for the future*—miscarriage and infertility; loss of a job and sense of worth; chronic debilitating illness.
- *Children's heartache*—e.g. loss of a parent, sibling, or pet; divorce.
- *Heartache chosen* in order to avoid even greater heartache in the future—as in ending a relationship that has become destructive even though there is pain and loss in doing so.

Likewise, the treatment menu can be tailored for different types of heartache. Some of the methods of treatment that primary physicians, once alerted to the presence of heartache, can help implement include:

- *Monitoring the patient* through telemetry of heart (a study of heart rhythm during everyday activities, which can be done from home) or home healthcare with hands-on monitoring of blood pressure as well as psychological well-being.

- *Introducing animal therapy.*
- *Activating a support group* to be present daily without offering excessive opinions or advice.
- *Alerting and encouraging interventions* from clergy or other spiritual mentors.
- *Prescribing medications* to help the patient with depression and anxiety make the transition to normal mood and behavior.
- *Helping the patient avoid or break unhealthy patterns* such as alcohol abuse and eating disorders.
- *Understanding* that heartache will most likely increase the perceived pain from a chronic condition such as arthritis and low back pain. (The primary physician or pain-medicine physician needs to help address this issue.)
- *Intervening psychologically* to break the cycles of chronic unresolved heartache.
- *Structuring a possible cardiac rehab program* to treat the heartache.
- *Educating about heartache*—could it be said that the most important part of a doctor-patient relationship is education? If you educate patients about what heartache is, including the physiological manifestations, they are much more likely to participate in the menu of treatments. They are also more likely to articulate the nature of the symptoms they are experiencing. When a doctor taps into a patient's inner knowing, and a patient taps into a doctor's medical knowledge, the two of those together make for a powerful combination.

7

How Can I Learn to Treat My Own Heartache?

The thing that causes our suffering is also causing our endurance,
which is bringing us hope.
—Robert K. Hudnut[32]

An operating room nurse with whom I work related the emotional highs and lows that she has experienced in her love relationship over the years. She asked:

> How can I better deal with the heartache rollercoaster? I know it affects me profoundly physically: I have weight gain, insomnia, depression, and a marked decrease in energy. Now I know some of the physiologic responses to my recurring heartache. Before, I always thought it was purely my emotional instability, but now I can plan physical conditioning and nutrition. Pairing that with

---

32 Robert K. Hudnut, *Meeting God in the Darkness* (Ventura, CA: Regal Books, 1989), p. 229.

maturity and a growing spiritual essence, I hope
to level out the peaks and valleys of my heartache
rollercoaster to some degree.

This courageous woman was addressing the question at the
center of this book: *"How can I learn to treat my own heartache?"*

For some, heartache accumulates slowly over years of
hurts and adverse experiences. For others who sustain sudden
shocks, the first question in treating their own heartache is,
"What do I do when I feel as if my chest is about to explode?"

The classic saying among those who teach courses in
cardiopulmonary life support is "the sooner you act, the less
likely you are to have irreparable damage to your heart."
Waiting while symptoms of a cardiac event get worse is *the*
biggest mistake patients make.

You shouldn't rush to the emergency room and announce
your impending heart attack due to temporary and minor
symptoms like feeling dizzy or winded. We know that intense
emotional states have physiological manifestations that are
not life threatening.

However, if you are feeling a definite physical change
in response to catastrophic news, then you should take this
situation extremely seriously. Any constellation of physical
sensations including pressure or pain in the chest, upper
abdomen, arms, or awareness that your heart is beating with
an irregular pulse rhythm is cause for *immediate* medical
monitoring.

Don't let embarrassment or intimidation keep you from
taking action. Go to the nearest urgent care facility and say

to them, "I'm having chest pain and I want to be evaluated for a cardiac event." Better yet, ask a family member or friend or coworker to drive you. If no one is around, call 911—that's why the system exists. Just get there—and get medical monitoring as soon as possible.

Err on the safe side. This is not a time to be proud and tough it out. If you are a loving parent and you know your child is in danger, you will not hesitate to act immediately in the best interests of your child's safety. Give your own care the same priority. Trust your instincts! At this point, they are just as valuable in determining a course of action as material data collected by medical professionals. If you wait too long, you might not ever get the chance to gather such data.

Consider these statistics: "The elevated risk of heart attack in the first twenty-four hours after loss of a loved one was fourteen times higher than normal. In the second twenty-four hours, eight times higher; in the third twenty-four hours, six times higher."[33] Remember: the sooner you act, the better your chances of treating the possible physical consequences of heartache.

Medical personnel are trained to evaluate chest pain and have a protocol they follow rapidly and urgently for the diagnosis and safety of the patient. This includes an electrocardiogram (EKG—a graphic demonstration of the heart's electrical pathways with normal and abnormal variants) and taking the five vital signs (blood pressure, pulse, respiration, body temperature, and level of pain). Often blood is drawn to evaluate cardiac enzymes. All urgent-care facilities are equipped to perform these evaluations. If any of these tests indicate that there is a cardiac problem, the next

33   M. Mittelman, "American Heart Association Conference on Cardiovascular Disease and Epidemiology," *Family Practice News* 26 (15 April 1996):8.

level of protocol is instituted. Typically, this happens at the same urgent-care facility. Most often, the patient is evaluated and can go home. If the situation is unclear, they will go to a higher level of testing.

For many people, heartbreaking news does *not* cause a feeling as if the chest is literally going to explode. There may be a sense of doom, sadness, anxiety, or a temporary unsteadiness, heaviness, and/or shortness of breath. It is wise to be attended by a dependable neighbor, friend, or family member who can monitor your emotional and physical state. Because this is a dynamic situation, it is not appropriate to be alone at such a time.

The consultation with a family physician or primary care provider can help with anti-anxiety and anti-depression medication. They are trained to observe the red-flag signs or changes that would indicate increasing the level of intervention.

Clergy and spiritual caregivers are trained to observe people who have had bad news. Seek such support to help decrease the acute heartbreak interval and to avoid chronic, untreated heartbreak. Prayer, meditation, and biofeedback relaxation—along with appropriate medication—can blunt the acute heartache.

Multiple studies have shown the presence of loving animals can soften the pain as well. Art and music therapy can ease the sting of heartache for many people. What therapy you choose to practice isn't as important as the fact that you choose solace from a menu of options. When I was preparing for mitral-valve repair surgery, I was greatly helped by the Quaker writer Richard Foster's excellent treatment of spiritual practices, *Celebration of Discipline*.[34] Others may find authors and mentors within their own traditions or from a variety of sources.

The Pueblo Indians of the Southwest, neighbors of the Navajos, have often thrived in two spiritual worlds, practicing the Roman Catholicism that was introduced to them centuries ago intermingled with their own animistic beliefs. Native Americans have a very pragmatic attitude toward healing. They have no qualms about mixing various healing ceremonies. They are humble in their willingness to try alternative methods of healing. In contrast to Western culture, which presumes that medical science and technology is the only route to recovery, Navajos easily accept the mystery that two entirely different treatments can work together to heal.

One of the problems with understanding heartache is that the conventional wisdom teaches that, given time, we are expected to "get over it." We're encouraged to go to support groups. But, words can be empty. We don't have any physiological understanding of what is happening during heartache, and therefore we lack a menu of therapeutic options.

How do you recognize that you're caught in an emotional and physical downward spiral of long-term heartache? It can be an insidious deterioration, so that low-grade depression becomes entrenched, and life feels devoid of hope and joy. You lose the bounce in your step and the twinkle in your eye without even realizing they're gone. If this sounds like you, run down the list of *"dragged down D's."* If one or more of them has become characteristic of your life, it is a sign you are struggling with depression and its fallout:

---

34   Richard J. Foster, *Celebration of Discipline: The Path to Spiritual Growth* (San Francisco: HarperSanFrancisco, 1988).

- *Deactivation*: decreased energy for exercise and healthy behaviors
- *Dependency*: reliance on others
- *Drug-seeking*: self-medicating
- *Deteriorating relationships*: withdrawing from others
- *Dormant spirituality*: decreased hunger for personal growth, diminished hope, and decreased interest in life in general

This downward process is like watching a plant grow—you don't see the changes every day—but over time you notice the differences. You're not aware that you are making this gradual descent, but you notice that the landscape of your life begins to look more and more like shades of gray.

As recovery begins, what signals that you're pulling out of the downward cycle? I call the emotional markers of moving beyond acute heartache the *"rebounding R's."* They are similar to recovery from long-term, chronic depression:

- *Reactivation:* paying attention to your physical well-being by reaching a goal with your exercise and weight; diligence of attending to your needs; establishing a pattern of working on your physical well-being that reflects consistent accomplishment.
- *Responsibility:* practicing self-reliance; celebrating an independent spirit by doing things on your own rather than depending on the assistance of others; practicing self-compassion when you fail or falter and self-praise for the courage to accept challenges. (Because you had to go to the hardware store four times to fix the toilet doesn't mean the process wasn't valuable. It's agonizing

to get stuck on the computer but gratifying to figure out the problem by yourself through perseverance.)

- *Re-creation:* creating ways to reduce dependency on pain medications; creating uses for discretionary time; pursuing alternatives to entrenched habits and behaviors.
- *Reaching out in relationships:* Who wants to go work out? Do it anyway. "Fake it till you make it!" The same principles operate to reconnect with people. You have to overcome resistance and put forth the effort to feel better. When social relationships are strengthened, you will be surprised how much more confident you will feel.
- *Reawakening:* exploring and nurturing your spiritual life; seeking your spiritual values goals and honoring them; taking classes in meditation or tai chi or yoga; permitting hope for the future.

I had a friend who lost an eighteen-year-old son to a motorcycle accident. Sara was a warm, affectionate lady, but after her son's death she developed a flat affect. People came by to visit, but she was not communicative. She stopped socializing and going to church. Gradually she simply lost the skills of relationship. As she avoided interactions with the people and the world around her, others began to avoid her.

Her husband was such a kind person that he enabled her withdrawal by doing essential tasks for her. He went grocery shopping, cooked all the meals, managed the finances, and made sure the housekeeping was done. She no longer left the house. She almost luxuriated in her isolation and indolence. By choosing not to feel and process her heartache, she cut herself off from feeling entirely.

Eventually, everyone around Sara realized that her withdrawal had become mental illness. She appeared to have premature aging and cognitive defects. Older people can choose to keep their minds active; Sara had allowed her cognitive skills to languish. She was diagnosed with premature dementia. After fifteen years, her basic needs required that she be admitted to a nursing home. She died at age sixty, literally having chosen to suspend life rather than cope with its disappointments.

Sara's case was a most extreme example of succumbing to heartache instead of treating it. Most chronic heartache sufferers descend into dysthymia—a chronic, yet functional, low-level depression. They may realize that life has subtly changed but are unaware that their engagement with life has diminished. They are not proactive in seeking to move beyond the "dragged-down D's."

Measure your engagement with life: if three years have passed and you have not resumed your usual life activities, then there is a chronicity occurring. It takes work to break through chronic depression; there may be some fits and starts. Is there a place you love that you can visualize to help you through the bleak moments when you're on the freeway and feel like you're smothering? A literal place you can go to find peace and quiet and beauty for your soul when you're in the midst of grief and loss?

A friend of mine created a spiritual "closet" in a corner of her house just big enough to sit down in. She created a screen to set off the corner from the rest of the room, put up black and white photos of cathedrals and added a prayer rug and a few sacred objects that gave her comfort. She had picked up a rock at a beautiful stream that felt just right when she held it in her hand, and she had bought a candleholder while visiting her favorite cathedral. At hand, she placed a prayer book she liked to use when she didn't have words of her own.

When life seems to shine again, don't lose the lifeline that pulled you back into it. Make conscious space in your life for the thoughts and behaviors that helped you pull out of chronic heartache.

In the ancient Pueblo Indian villages in the heartland of New Mexico, the Feast Day dances have been part of the rhythm of life for over a thousand years. Lines of dancers dressed in traditional, colorful animal representations respond in unison to the chorus of drummers and chanters. From behind an adobe house appears an old man painted in black and white stripes. He is the Kashake or Kosas—a spiritual guide and healer. But on Feast Day this exalted figure is referred to as a clown.

This seems like a strange contrast, almost a contradiction. How could a deeply respected healer be considered a clown? Because he, of all people, is well acquainted with the weaknesses and ironies that lie just under the surface of everyday life. Like all clowns, he takes on an exaggerated representation of these realities. And so he wanders playfully through the village and its dancers, joking and exposing secrets. Many of these secrets are lingering heartache from broken relationships or hidden pain. When they are brought to the surface in the midst of a communal and sacred ceremony, the heartache is brought into the light in order to begin the process of healing.

In ancient societies, the pain of heartache is acknowledged as an inevitable reality of our human experience. In our technologically proficient culture, pain is something to be feared and medicated away; heartache tends to be marginalized and stigmatized. Lacking rituals to deal with it, we find it an uncomfortable disruption of life.

The process of bringing heartache out of hiding can be profoundly therapeutic. It can save lives. It can ease the terrible pain of acute grief. It can decrease long-term consequences of heartache.

The most important action step in the wake of heartache is taking charge of your own healing. Patients can perform some or all of the following items for themselves. In the acute phase of heartache, consider these practical steps:

- *Be alert to your physical symptoms.* Pay particular attention to the following symptoms: chest pain, a heavy feeling or pounding in the chest, skipped heartbeats, shortness of breath, profuse sweating, nausea and vomiting, an impending feeling of doom, and an abrupt change in your sense of well-being.
- *Know how to react proactively* should these physical symptoms be present. Call for help from a friend or relative and consider calling 911 or being taken to the emergency room or urgent care.
- *Identify an advocate* who can help you institute medical care for any health situation, but in particular for potentially dangerous circumstances such as acute heartache.
- *Exercise or move your body* in any way that your physical health permits. A short walk in the outdoors stimulates

mind, body, and senses. If is difficult not to feel some life force when surrounded by the animals, plants, sun, and sky.

- *Ask for spiritual support* if you have a faith-based value system. For many, turning a seemingly impossible problem over to a higher source gives hope and "the peace that passes all understanding" at a time of great risk, sadness, and anxiety.
- *Blunt the acute signs and symptoms of heartache by asking for emotional help and physical closeness from friends and family.*
- *Delay or delegate any activities that require increased motor skills or alertness,* such as driving or operating machinery.
- *Avoid making major decisions.*
- *Avoid activities that decrease cognitive skills,* such as drinking alcohol or taking non-prescription or recreational drugs.

The key is learning to live with heartache in a way that leads to renewal instead of despondency. This may be a major change in perception and behavior. Change is not cozy, but the most fertile time for growth is during a crisis. Pain and anxiety motivate the desire for change. It is important to move through the stages of grief and not short-circuit the authenticity of your process to suit another's timetable.

Here is a testimony from a participant in the American Cancer Society's Cancer Survivor's Network. After treatment for her illness, she was blindsided by a wall of heartache. Notice what kinds of interventions she pursued and what kind of advice she gives:

After nine months of treatment, barreling through the best I could, I gave birth to a massive monster of grief. Looking back, I can see that I had so much stuff to process. With friends' support, counseling, meditation, yoga, prayer, and medication I can now look back and see the monster for what it was and is. It took from October until July for me to finally wake up from what felt like a nightmare...I am a slow learner, so it took me a long while to see the help I needed and to process what needed to be processed. This is what I've learned: Seek help. What you are experiencing is NOT uncommon and not to be minimized. You will feel better. You do not need to apologize for how you feel. [35]

Eventually, heartache is everyone's problem. It is as common as the cold or the flu and can be as devastating as a heart attack. To feel fragile physically and emotionally—and to admit it—takes courage. To hide from heartache due to denial or fear of weakness can risk life itself. It can prolong *acute* heartache and possibly lead to *chronic long-term* heartache. The pain of heartache can be shortened and blunted with support. A reawakened spirit and a new vigor for life lie on the other side of heartache.

Participate in your own wellness. Because you're experiencing heartache does not mean you are a sick person. You're a well person with heartache. It's important to take action. Heartache need not deteriorate into psychological or physical illness.

---

35   "Lynn," from the Cancer Survivors Network discussion board on "grieving and depression," http://csn.cancer.org/node/175942, downloaded September 19, 2009 - 1:49pm.

8

WHY ARE PETS SO CLOSELY ASSOCIATED WITH HEARTACHE?

No wonder we love our animals so much, owe them so much, and wish so fervently that they will be with us always. The soul of a dog is its faithfulness, its friendship, its comfort.
—Jon Katz[36]

At a dinner with friends, our conversation turned to the recent death of one man's mother. I knew this woman because I had performed some procedures to ease her back pain as she battled chronic obstructive pulmonary disease. To get along with this woman was not easy for her son. She kept herself bound up so tightly with her health concerns that she had little energy for relationships, and she kept her son at an emotional distance.

Not long before his mother died, this man had also lost a beloved pet—a dog he'd had for over twelve years. The dog had been like a family member. "I feel guilty that my dog's death was harder on me than my mother's death," he

36 Jon Katz, *Soul of a Dog: Reflections on the Spirits of the Animals of Bedlam Farm* (New York: Random House, 2010), p. 161.

commented. "It sounds terrible to say, but I actually had a much closer relationship with my dog. Even though I loved her, and in her later years understood why she was so emotionally absent in my life, I got much more comfort from my dog than I ever received from my mother."

Pet lovers experience a special bond with their animals that can be described as a heartfelt connection. Those who are not pet lovers are often puzzled by the intensity of this bond. When it is broken by the animal's death, the loss is felt at a primal level. Compared to human relationships, it is an uncluttered loss—just heartache, pure and simple, without the thousand regrets or ambivalence or questioning that often accompanies human relationships.

In the power of animals to build up our sense of self and make us feel loved, there is the corresponding potential to make us feel a sense of loss that is surprisingly personal—as if no one else could understand what that pet added to our life. Losing a beloved animal is a peculiarly direct blow to the heart.

Sadly, my friend received more personal validation from his dog than from his emotionally unavailable mother. How many of us flee the complication of human relationships for the relative safety of animals? They provide a unique connection that buffers heartache, although their usually shorter life spans may make us vulnerable to their loss.

Animals have a surprising power to reach our hearts directly; the bond feels more like a heart to heart, intuitive knowing of our essential selves. The only time it is distorted is when the animal's psyche or spirit has been damaged by human abuse.

Nursing homes and hospices have long recognized the unconditional, uncomplicated love that animals provide. The soft touch of a loving animal can put a sparkle back into eyes that have otherwise grown dull from illness and isolation. What an antidote for the decreasing life forces of the hospice patient or nursing home resident!

In 2007, Dr. David Dosa, a geriatrician, wrote about the astonishing behavior of a cat that lived at a nursing and rehabilitation center in Providence, Rhode Island. With an unerring sense of which patient was about to die, Oscar would curl up on the bed next to that person, staying there until shortly after he or she passed. His behavior was so predictable that nurses knew to call loved ones when Oscar made his move.

Dosa describes an incident in which a priest was giving last rites while Oscar lay next to the patient, purring and gently nuzzling her:

> A young grandson asks his mother, "What is the cat doing here?" The mother, fighting back tears, tells him, "He is here to help Grandma get to heaven." Thirty minutes later, Mrs. K. takes her last earthly breath. With this, Oscar sits up, looks around, then departs the room so quietly that the grieving family barely notices.[37]

---

37   David M. Dosa, MD, MPH., "A Day in the Life of Oscar the Cat," *The New England Journal of Medicine* (26 July 2007), no. 4, 357:329. Dosa went on to write a book entitled *Making Rounds with Oscar: The Extraordinary Gift of an Ordinary Cat* (New York: Hyperion, 2010).

Oscar is just one compelling example of the ways in which animals are intuitively attuned to our emotional and physical states. Writer Jon Katz describes the hospice volunteer visits he made with his border collie, Izzy, a dog exquisitely attuned to the varying needs of the people they met—including those with Alzheimer's—patients who were otherwise hardest to reach. "Nothing I saw was more mysterious or moving than the emotions dogs can evoke, their capacity to help heal us," he writes:

> All winter, Izzy and I went in and out of houses and trailers and nursing homes, visiting people who were dying, and their families. And a practice that began as an impulse to do something good with my dog evolved into something much more, an excursion into the enigmatic realm of dogs and healing. All kinds of people—rich and poor, educated and not, clearheaded and mired in pain—believed that Izzy could, not cure them, but make them feel more peaceful, loved, cared for.[38]

Although much of the information surrounding animal-assisted therapy is anecdotal, there are studies supporting the anecdotal evidence with solid research. For example, researchers in St. Louis studied the effects of therapy dogs on elderly patients in a long-term care facility. They found that as little as a half-hour each week with a therapy dog significantly reduced

---

38   Jon Katz, *Izzy and Lenore* (New York: Villard, 2008), p. 187.

loneliness after only six weeks of such activity.[39] James Lynch and Aaron Katcher, MD, were among the first to demonstrate how pets helped patients recover from heart attacks. Those without pet companions were much more likely to die in the first year following their heart attack than those with pets.

Clearly, animals have a unique power to mitigate the effects of isolation and illness. Scientists have established a neurochemical basis for this bonding. When we engage in physical affection with animals, the brain releases a hormone responsible for bonding—the "love hormone"—called oxytocin.[40] This physiological response supports and reinforces the emotional response for which we seem to be hard-wired.

Of course, the heartache that animals can alleviate by their presence can also be triggered by their absence. Animal lovers all know the heartache associated with losing a loyal dog or a loving cat. The physical consequences and risk of this heartache are greater in the aging population. Many elderly people focus their life around a pet. Their contacts, activities, and energy level revolve around the needs of the pet. With the death of the loving dog or cat they are at risk for negative physical consequences and even sudden death from heartache. Realization of this increased risk can help relatives, friends, and healthcare workers watch for and appropriately treat the physiological and psychological changes caused by heartache in the elderly.

---

39   Banks, Marian R. and William A. Banks. "The Effects of Animal-Assisted Therapy on Loneliness in an Elderly Population in Long-Term Care Facilities." Journal of Gerontology: Medical Sciences 57A.7 (2002): M428-M432.

40   See, for example, Meg Daley Olmert, *Made for Each Other: The Biology of the Human-Animal Bond* (New York: Da Capo Press, 2010).

Emmit was an eighty-year-old patient who would come to the Pain and Spine Center accompanied by his service dog: a Labrador-mix named Buddy. Emmit was wheelchair-bound from rheumatoid arthritis. Buddy helped Emmit with daily tasks and provided him with constant loving companionship.

I learned that Emmit and his now deceased wife had three very successful adult children who lived in London, Mumbai, and New York City. From all I could learn they had each enjoyed an active, healthy childhood. Their early years were filled with soccer, ballet, baseball, music camp, and active social lives. They had all attended excellent colleges and graduate schools at Emmit's expense. But their communication with their father gradually decreased to a hurried, obligatory, monthly phone call. Only one son visited him occasionally. Emmit talked frequently about his children and seemed to love them genuinely and eagerly anticipate news from them. He was certainly proud of their accomplishments. But his daily support and affection came entirely from Buddy. Although it appeared that Emmit had a "successful family," in reality it represented the dysfunctional nuclear family unit that has become all too familiar. Even though there were no obvious family conflicts, there was minimal contact and support.

The nurses in The Pain and Spine Center read of Emmit's passing in the newspaper obituary. We learned that Buddy had died unexpectedly a week prior to Emmit's death. We assumed the physical consequences of heartache might have led to Emmit's death. Considering the love they shared, it is a likely assumption.

In this technologically advanced society many elderly people crave contact with family, and the television seems a weak substitute. The adult children are geographically elsewhere. Perhaps the old adage "out of sight, out of mind" applies. Sometimes older people turn to the unconditional loyalty and love of an animal. As life becomes contracted for senior citizens, there is often a very scanty support system to help them endure the heartache that comes from the loss of a loving pet. This is a precarious time for the physical health of the elderly. This may be the end, or the beginning of the end, for them. Doctors, nurses, family, and friends need to be proactive to ensure that physical and emotional support is available to avert a tragic event such as death or organ damage.

Whether it is birds, cats, dogs, horses, dolphins and whales, chimpanzees and silverback gorillas, or even elephants— stories of our bonding with animals run the gamut of the animal kingdom. They touch our hearts deeply and uniquely. Even the pharaohs of ancient Egypt chose to go into the life hereafter with their dearest pets. Animal mummies from ancient Egyptian dynasties reveal the complex relationships Egyptians had with animals. Animals had significance not only for physical sustenance and spiritual veneration but also for companionship. Dogs and cats were buried with their masters—one mummy in the Egyptian Museum in Cairo shows that even a commoner "was laid to rest with his small dog curled up at his feet."[41] Over the centuries, societies have recognized the power of animals to ease human suffering and to be our companions in the struggles and joys of life. Our heartache over the passing of beloved animal companions is exceeded only by the gifts of the heart they bring to us.

---

41   A. R. William, "Animals Everlasting," *National Geographic* (November 2009), vol. 216:no. 5, p. 38.

9

WHAT DOES THE PROCESS OF RECOVERY LOOK LIKE?

Your soul is not a passive or a theoretical entity that occupies a space in the vicinity of your chest cavity. It is a positive, purposeful force at the core of your being.
—Gary Zukav[42]

Just as treating heart disease is critical to avoiding further complications or sudden death, so heartache needs treating in order to avoid its own array of complications. "Recovery" from heartache is not, strictly speaking, an accurate term, because we never really get over heartache; rather, we get on with life. So "recovering" from heartache is more like learning to live with chronic pain—there is healing, but there is no cure.

The consequences of untreated heartache were vividly illustrated in the life of a friend of mine who was a very successful businessman. Al worked in the snow-skiing industry in the 1970s, '80s, and '90s—periods of phenomenal

42   Gary Zukav, *The Seat of the Soul* (New York: Fireside/Simon & Schuster, 1989), p. 31.

growth. In the prime of his life, Al was married with two children. Everything seemed to be going his way.

After an unexpected divorce, he buried his emotional turmoil by increasing the frenetic pace of his life. Rather than trying to find support and take care of himself physically, he plunged into an "exciting" way of life, which, as it turned out, included elevated blood pressure. This in turn led to severe physical consequences: a stroke with paraplegia and some difficulty talking. He was a picture of what it looks like when recovery from heartache is postponed. The consequences are profoundly destructive.

Al and I had been good friends in high school. When we reconnected later in life, I was struck by his courage in trying to find meaningful experiences in spite of his paraplegia and decreased verbal skills. There he was, showing all of us how to deal with adversity.

I took Al to the cabin where I have been writing this book. Near the foot of Wolf Creek Pass, Colorado, and above a sparkling stretch of the San Juan River, we discussed his struggles with the "dragged-down D's": diminished hope, deactivation, dependency, drug-seeking, deteriorating relationships, and dormant spirituality. At the river's edge, we formed a metaphor for our discussion of life and its often-turbulent flow. A river flows from its headwaters to its eventual dispersion into the ocean just as our physical selves make a winding journey from birth to our eventual dissolution and return to the elements. Al finds hope for the future by reconnecting with friends from his past. These relationships provide diversion and depth to his life. Such connections, celebrations, and reunions yield opportunities that create a hopeful future.

Although he needs a cane and sometimes a wheelchair, Al goes to the gym nearly every day. With help from physical therapists and a trainer, he has created a modified workout that has propelled him from *deactivated* to *reactivated*.

Al now works part-time and is involved in a California state planning commission for the disabled. Although he is dependent on others for many things, he prides himself in the independent actions he never thought possible before he entered rehabilitation.

As we watched the river flow by, Al asked me about my spiritual beliefs and discussed his Buddhist background. Although he did not share any spiritual epiphany, the discussion itself seemed to awaken him from spiritual dormancy. To celebrate our renewed friendship, we have made plans to visit the Napa Valley wine country near his home.

Al's story is inspiring to me, but it also highlights the importance of attending to heartache rather than ignoring it. Are there issues in our lives we need to address in order to avoid negative consequences on the heart? Can we proactively prepare for the frequently dangerous physical changes of acute heartache? Can we learn to modulate acute heartache with emotional and spiritual strength training?

Medically speaking, what can we learn from cardiac rehab about treating heartache? The American Heart Association defines cardiac rehab as "a medically supervised program to help heart patients recover quickly" from a cardiac event.[43]

---

43   From the website of the American Heart Association, "Cardiac Rehabilitation," http://www.americanheart.org/presenter.jhtml?identifier=4490.

Clinical trials indicate that such programs help heart patients improve their overall physical, mental, and social function.

Cardiac rehab is an ideal arena for people suffering both acute and chronic heartache, especially those at increased risk for a cardiac event (due to obesity, high blood pressure, advanced age, diabetes, abnormal serum cholesterol values, smoking, family history of heart disease, and previous cardiac dysfunction).

Rehab programs are designed to improve the health of the physical organ by increasing blood flow to the heart, stimulating revascularization around scar tissue (growth of new vessels to replace the old, clogged ones), decreasing blood pressure, and improving the entire cardiovascular system to make it run as efficiently as possible. For heartache sufferers, these programs may facilitate a progression from vulnerability to vitality—both physically and emotionally.

Heartache patients can participate in all or part of the following resources of cardiac rehabilitation:

- *Education about cardiac rehab* and why it is wise and appropriate treatment for heartache.
- *Guided exercise programs* that are individually tailored to work around physical limitations. Exercise releases "endogenous" (created inside the body)—morphine-like substances that provide a sense of physical and psychological well-being. In rehab, the exercise level is gradually increased while monitoring the heart's response.
- *Nutrition education* and how diet relates to cardiac risk and body dysfunction. Most people need a powerful motivating force to commit to changes in eating and exercise habits. The pain of heartache may be that force,

when supported by the atmosphere of wellness in a rehab program that is designed to improve nutritional habits.

- *Information about the potential physiological dangers of heartache* (for example, catecholamine surge and diminished ejection fraction) that lead to cardiac dysfunction and even death.
- *Counseling about the use of medications.* On a temporary basis, anti-anxiety and anti-depressant medications can blunt the emotional response to acute heartache. Other medications can be used to control blood pressure and stabilize cardiac function and irregular heart rhythms.
- *Group therapy and individual counseling can be accomplished in an exercise environment* that is not as intrusive and contrived as the sterile clinical office setting. The flow of emotional support can be more unobtrusive and natural when people are concentrating on health rather than on illness. Focusing on illness too often can lead to "woundology," a side-effect phenomenon in which people contest for who has the greatest medical problems.[44] Ironically, the wounds themselves become a source of identity and a paradoxical measure of self-worth.

The steps in cardiac rehab form a framework for patients to shape a healthy lifestyle made up of new commitments and progressively established habits. Ideally, after the rehab program is finished, patients continue with a plan for daily exercise.

---

44   See the origin of this term in Carolyn Myss, Ph.D., *Why People Don't Heal and How They Can* (NY: Three Rivers Press, 1997), p. 6.

Developing and maintaining a routine of appropriate activity should be as automatic as brushing the teeth. Most people do not have the discipline to maintain a daily exercise program without designating a habitual time and place for it. They also do not have the knowledge to change their exercises to avoid boredom and muscle memory. The same exercises done repeatedly over time are less effective physiologically than challenging the muscles and cardiovascular system with a new mixture of movements. An instructor or trainer can inspire, encourage, and motivate. The rehab program can recommend a combination of body movement programs such as Pilates, yoga, weight training, cycling, warm-water exercises, or swimming. Tailored for the individual needs of each patient, these programs can help transpose a patient's focus from illness to wellness.

Mending the heart is a creative process that should be in harmony with the stage of heartache you find yourself in. Get help in identifying where you are in the process of grief and assessing your menu of options. To locate an appropriate cardiac rehab program, get an order from your doctor and take it to a local rehab center.

You can take the rehab concept and broaden it to other spheres of life—such as the spiritual arena. In our pain center we take a multi-disciplinary approach, incorporating faith-based support along with medical, emotional, and psychological resources.

I remember a patient of mine who finally found the love of his life at age fifty. The couple married and settled into a rewarding life together. He was even happier in his work, which he attributed to his newly fulfilled life. To his great sorrow, however, within just a few years his wife was diagnosed with a brain tumor. Only two months after the diagnosis, she was dead.

Soon after, he began experiencing chest pain. He was diagnosed with angina, and he underwent coronary artery bypass surgery. Following his surgery, he enrolled in a cardiac rehab program and finished it successfully. Despite post-op indications that he was recuperating well, he continued to be bothered by chest pain on a daily basis. He was afraid he would either die from the pain or need further surgery.

It was his rabbi who finally helped him identify the source of the continuing pressure in his chest: heartache. Once he began differentiating this heartache from losing his beloved wife from the angina he no longer had, his fear gradually subsided. But the pain of heartache continued, for which no bypass surgery was available.

The antidote to the pain in his heart proved to be, in part, a rekindled spiritual awareness. He'd had a spiritual sensitivity in his youth but had lost it in the journey through adulthood. Now the boy had come back to visit the man, and the spiritual nurture was life restoring. It gave him strength simply to endure the heartache until in time and by grace, the ache gradually eased. Though the process was painfully slow, his heartache eventually diminished enough to allow him once again to find periods of light and joy.

If it doesn't catch up with us in our daily routines, heartache will inevitably come calling in the lonely hours of the night. If we suppress it there as well, it will likely come back to visit us in mental and physical distress, as my friend Al experienced.

Of course, not all healing from heartache is measurable, particularly in the emotional realm. Still, there are ways of discerning where one is in the recovery process. I have learned much from my pain patients, but I can attest from personal experience to the particular pain of the heartsick.

First, *let heartache enlarge your life instead of shrinking it.* When it strikes, you may feel that if you do not get relief from it immediately, it will take over your life or end your life. Although the heartache may well give you a new picture of your future, it need not dictate your future. It does not have the power to define you. It can lead to a life larger than you had planned by opening up new boundaries, but only if you choose to step outside and do something different to awaken your energies in defiance of the defeat that heartache insinuates upon you.

Second, *allow hopelessness to lead you to hope.* Once all conventional sources of help have been exhausted, the work of the spirit begins in earnest. This is the path that leads beyond despair to a discovery of something higher and deeper as a source of meaning and purpose. Some people are innately able to walk the fragile ground between despair and hope. For others it is too difficult, and they need guidance and support to move beyond hopelessness.

Writer Philip Yancey defines hope as "simply the belief that something good lies ahead. It is not the same as optimism or wishful thinking, for these imply a denial of reality."[45] Heartache sufferers have already had many hopes ripped out of their grasp. They know all too well what has failed them as a trustworthy source of hope, but they need not live in that failure: they have

---

45   Philip Yancey, *Where Is God When It Hurts?* (Grand Rapids: Zondervan, 1990), p. 210.

an opportunity to redefine the "good" in life. I have seen over and over again that those who seek *will* find.

Third, *embrace mystery while seeking answers.* Some pain seems easier to bear if we think we know why it happened or what purpose it will serve. Even bad answers seem preferable to no answers. The problem is that these "answers" can short-circuit the healing process in a kind of arrested development.

The paradox of heartache is that it is likely to take from you the meaning you thought you needed and replace it with a meaning you could not have anticipated. You will never get a satisfactory answer to the plea, "Why is this experience happening to me?" But you may be propelled into a new way of looking at your life with the question, "How is this experience teaching me about what is most important in my life?"

Fourth, *accept the crucible of transformation.* I have found that the wisest spiritual guides tend to be people who have learned to live with pain. They do not spout shallow advice. These individuals model for me a way of walking through darkness, but they cannot learn my lessons for me. The only way I can acquire the wisdom of experience is the hard way.

Heartache exacts a great price, but it can also yield a great return: transformation. You may not have the ability to change the circumstances of your suffering, but you do have the ability to choose how you will respond to those circumstances. For some, this choice may be the only path of release.

Fifth, *practice gratitude amid loss.* Most people think that recovery means regaining what was damaged by illness or injury. Since heartache often involves irretrievable loss, we think there is never going to be any recovery. But just because life is irrevocably altered, it doesn't mean that life is at an end. We now have to forge a different way of life, and we may find that the new beginning is more significant than the way we had been living. For this new beginning, we can practice gratitude.

Dr. Frank Vertosick describes this discovery of gratitude in the life of a woman with intractable face pain:

> [She] enjoyed counseling other victims of face pain so much that she began to see her own illness in a different light. Without personally experiencing the disease, she would never have had the opportunity to minister to others. She found meaning in an otherwise meaningless malady and came to see it as a blessing. In a sense, she was cured, not by craniotomy but by a restructuring of her attitude.[46]

Loss has a way of forcing us to give up our personal agendas. When we stop making demands for what we want, we will have room to acknowledge what we have.

Sixth, *recognize that wholeness comes through brokenness.* Heartache forces us to confront our vulnerability. We come face to face with a broken spirit that feels inadequate to cope with the loss we have suffered. This kind of brokenness hurts far worse than virtually any physical pain that most of us will face in a lifetime.

But the drive to heal is just as strong in the human spirit as it is in the human body—perhaps stronger. Just as the body has marvelous ways of overcoming injury and is always striving to recover a sense of physical wholeness, so inwardly the human spirit is striving to heal heartache and recover that innate sense of wholeness.

---

46   Frank T. Vertosick, Jr., *Why We Hurt: The Natural History of Pain* (New York: Harcourt, 2000), p. 278.

When suffering is transformed from meaningless loss to a redefined meaning and purpose, wholeness no longer depends on that impossible dream of recovering what has been lost. Instead, it arises from the recognition that what happens in our heart is more powerful than what happens in our circumstances. It is felt in the inner peace of accepting that external losses can give us a greater awareness of what elements truly center our lives.

10

What Are the Most Important Insights for Learning to Live with Heartache?

The world's pain does break our hearts, over and over and over again, but a broken heart is not a paralyzed one...hearts are broken open, not destroyed; and from an open heart's capacity to be with suffering, healing arises.
—Elizabeth Roberts and Elias Amidon[47]

Novelist Gail Godwin writes of C. S. Lewis that when he was grief-stricken by the death of his wife, it shattered not only his heart but also the emotional shell he had been living inside for much of his life:

> What makes *A Grief Observed* so much more than a "grief book," even a grief book by a man of

---

47   Elizabeth Roberts and Elias Amidan, *Prayers for a Thousand Years* (San Francisco: HarperSanFrancisco, 1999), pp. 50-51.

spirit and intellect accustomed to making words
do his bidding, is its fully *alive* quality. The
short, agonized endearments and entreaties,
the sharp arguments with God, the achingly
detailed catalog of just how much has been lost
for good, all exemplify the unsettling paradox
that one must be completely alive to completely
experience heartbreak. Heartbreak, in *A Grief
Observed,* is an amalgam of despair and elation, of
realizing that one is awake enough to experience
it fully. Though heartbreak permeates his life in
every line, *it has a vitality of its own.*[48]

Maybe it's unwise to wish the pain of heartache would
go away entirely. There is an ambivalence of wanting the
heartache to go away, yet not wanting it to disappear. In the
case of the loss of a child, memories are bittersweet. But
there may be great value in anticipating dreams or memories
of a lost relationship or of a deceased loved one. These images
often occur in night dreams or daydreams and can be peaceful
or disturbing. Part of us waits anxiously for them; part of us
dreads their recurrence. Reframing memories and dreams of
loved ones from triggers of heartache to positive messages
that celebrate the goodness of the relationship eases anguish
and gives substance to heartache.

A smile on the street or in a café trips the sensory
neuropathways to recreate a scene in which the lost person
is momentarily present again. This can restart the flood
of desperate feelings, even years after the loss. Most of us
learn to rein in this cascade of feelings so we can move on

---

48   Gail Godwin, *Heart: A Personal Journey Through Its Myths and Meanings* (New York: William Morrow, 2001), pp. 174-75.

with the day. It is, at the least, mood-dampening for a while. But although these unexpected daggers of loss are painful, we would be poorer without them because they are vivid reminders of a loved one, and the happiness they gave us.

I choose to think that during these glimpses of the past, those who have gone before us are tapping us over the heart. My son's godmother, Dora Tse Pe from San Ildefonso Indian Pueblo, breaks a little piece of bread off before each meal to honor the loved ones who have left their physical bodies. She talks to them as if they were as close as her shadow. They are ever present to her.

In the midst of acute heartache, we can hardly breathe much less imagine "moving on"—the annoying cliché that implies we can get past grief. But through grace ("gratuitous goodness" or "undeserved favor") there is usually a healing. The scars and some pain remain always. But we add these scars to our essence and move toward the lighted way before us. This process of illumination from severe adversity is a gift. This helps us descend from the troubled thoughts of the mind and its constant chatter into the inner chambers of the heart.

The Russian mystic, Theophan the Recluse, said "To pray is to descend with the mind into the heart, and there to stand before the face of the Lord, ever-present, all seeing, within you."[49]

In acceptance, lies the peace that passes all understanding.

American society still clings to the notion that if you live right, you can somehow avoid heartache; and if you have

49   *The Art of Prayer: An Orthodox Anthology*, ed. Timothy Ware (London: Faber & Faber, 1966), p. 110.

heartache, you must have done something wrong. We deny its inevitability with the illusion that we have control over the events and passages of our lives. A better goal is not to avoid heartache but to focus on moving from untreated to treated heartache. All of us live with residual heartache. Some of it is private, but some of it is more externally driven—for example, the constant pressure of the physically challenged among us to function within a society set up for the able-bodied. Their longing for the freedom of a healthy body is a form of chronic heartache that is too often ignored rather than validated and addressed.

For all of us, to live with vitality at any level is to risk the recurrence of heartache. It is not only possible; it is likely. Now we are aware of its physical dangers: catecholamine surges that ask the heart to work harder...because such surges reduce the oxygen flow to the heart, the heart has less of what it needs to do that work...decreased ejection fraction, which lessens blood flow to the body organs, including the heart, from as high as 55 percent to as low as 15 percent, which may cause organ damage—whether to heart, kidney, or brain. For some people, these consequences can be deadly. Others will suffer chronic health conditions: depression, heart attacks with residual heart muscle damage, eating disorders, and other issues. For all, there is no returning to the way it was before. Rather, we are confronted with the reality of our "new normal."

Given the risk factors for both acute and chronic heartache, the medical community needs to ask the question on a routine basis. Although this is the art of practicing medicine, it also involves the science of evidence-based considerations—because heartache can lead to a cascade of obvious medical problems treatable with current medications.

If you are facing heartache as a complicating factor with another medical condition, consider taking an advocate with you to the doctor. When you are experiencing an emotional trauma with physical consequences, it's hard to receive and remember all the medical information you need in order to make decisions. An advocate can be any person who is less emotionally involved and can be your support by relaying information to the physician and afterwards summarizing for you what the physician said and helping you decide how to apply it. Frequently, patients come to our pain center with somebody who is writing down the information so that later on, the patient and advocate can reflect together on that information. An advocate can bridge the gap between the emotionality of the patient and the science of the doctor.

The challenge in meeting with a doctor is to get his or her attention about the reality of your heartache so that you can explore together the realities of both the medical and psychological impacts. Don't wait for physicians to add heartache to their review of symptoms. Participate in your own wellness as an act of self-advocacy.

As you know more, you may be able to be the instigator in a gentle and non-intrusive way, helping someone move from vulnerability to vitality by suggesting the adoption of proactive pathways of recovery.

In most physical injuries, the body slowly and imperceptibly heals itself. Occasionally healing does not occur, leaving chronic, weeping wounds or an injury that ultimately proves fatal. In similar fashion, most heartache is gradually healed albeit not necessarily cured. Cure implies no residual physical or emotional scars from the injury. Healing is a process of repair and change that allows the injured person to continue to function—but not without a cellular memory of the injury or some physical change. Healing can be compensatory and expansive, offering new insight and incentive for creative adaptation.

In my own life, I know that a recurrence of heartache would bring to the surface that dark tunnel of despair. Should that happen, I would find comfort in turning my heartache over to a higher spiritual source. I would hope to have the courage to look through the twin lenses of physical and emotional heartache and ask for help to begin interdisciplinary treatment options.

I have noticed that illness and pain often compel patients to find their own authentic faith. This, in turn, can lead to renewed relationships and greater transparency in relationships with loved ones. It seems that some energizing of the spirit is necessary to move from being entrenched in heartache to renewal in the midst of it.

This was certainly the case with Martha, a forty-four-year-old woman dying of adenocarcinoma of the lung, a malignancy found in only about 7 percent of total lung cancer cases. Martha's affluent family had been able to afford experimentation with a multitude of alternative treatment therapies. Following her lung biopsy they had pursued macrobiotic therapy in California and from there went to Mexico for even more non-traditional care. Martha's husband was a strong advocate of psychology-based approaches to defeating illnesses, such as meditation techniques and intentional thought processes. When they learned about the variety of alternative practices available in Santa Fe, he championed the family's move.

Sadly, before long Martha was admitted to the hospital emergency room in extreme pain. When I arrived, they were discussing pain medication. Martha was anxious, confused, and exhausted. Although her husband disapproved of pharmacological methods for handling his wife's pain, he began to relent. We started treatment with different kinds of oral narcotics, anti-emetics (for nausea), and patches placed on the skin to act as long-acting narcotic reservoirs to manage her physical pain.

As soon as her husband left the room, Martha turned to me and begged for help. I held her hand and listened to the person inside the wasting body. We talked about her pain and fear and her desire for a sense of peace. We reflected on how our lives are brief and transient moments in the span of existence. Pain brings us to our knees, giving us the opportunity to look toward eternity.

After about three of our sessions together, Martha eventually identified that deep within her was a profound heartache about the loss of her relationship with her mother. During this last stage of her life Martha found clarity about the need for reconciliation with her mother, to find peace, and to gain some closure. Even though there was no cure for her adenocarcinoma, there was a healing of chronic heartache.

Martha's intense anxiety began to drain away as peace welled up from within. With her mother, husband, and two sons by her side, joy and sorrow intermingled as wonderful reunion moments took place in her room in the midst of suffering. Her husband had become much more accepting of the benefits of Western medicine, and her family approached the reality of her impending death with a sense of peace and purpose.

Material comfort sometimes breeds the illusion that we can skate comfortably along the surface of life from one pleasant destination to the next. When the ice cracked open for Martha, she had a lot of work to do. She had ignored her heartache until all else fell away, and the spiritual was the only realm that held any hope for her. This eleventh-hour change opened up a larger world that gave new meaning to her life while she was preparing to leave it. She was able to reach deep down within to the fragments of belief and come up with the recrudescence of what was true for her, guiding her to a powerful sense of peace. Just as anxiety markedly accentuates heartache, so peacefulness markedly inhibits its intensity.

Time and again I have seen this peacefulness in the lives of patients who have chosen healthy ways of addressing their heartache rather than resisting or denying it.

Many of us have estranged relationships with family members, friends, and lovers. This is a chronic heartache caused not by the death of a loved one but by the loss of relationship. All parties are too proud or injured to seek out renewed communication. It is difficult for us to revisit the wounds of chronic, festering heartache.

But healing from heartache involves love and interpersonal relationships. Dean Ornish, MD, a pioneer in studies of the role of love and intimacy in health, has declared these factors so important that "I am not aware of any other factor—not diet, not smoking, not exercise, not stress, not genetics, not drugs, not surgery—that has a greater impact on our quality of life, incidence of illness, and premature death from all causes."[50]

It has been many years since my days as an anesthesiologist for open-heart procedures, many decades since my own repaired heart valve began to function well, and six years since Ellie died. I have moved far beyond viewing the heart through the lens of hard science, seeing it merely as a mechanical pump. My expanded relationship with the heart as a doctor, a patient, and a father has helped focus the twin lenses of evidence-based medicine and intuitive wisdom on the gracious reality of healing from heartache.

In the cardiovascular labs of institutions such as Johns Hopkins, the physicality of this healing has now been documented. The phenomenon of broken heart syndrome has done for the general public what my patients have done for me: it has brought heartache out of hiding.

A patient who arrived in my office at the end of a long day brought the hidden nature of heartache home to me recently. Instead of dragging in with a whimpering demeanor, he bounced in appearing as if he were an athlete in training. His problem was axial (low) back pain, but his X-rays were normal.

At this point in my day I was too tired to mince words, so I simply said to him, "The way you present is not like the usual pain patient. What is your real reason for coming?"

"Oh, you must be a doctor with a lot of intuition," he replied. He was an attractive man, about seventy-five pounds

50   Dean Ornish, *Love & Survival: 8 Pathways to Intimacy and Health* (New York: HarperCollins, 1998), pp. 2-3.

overweight. "I've had liposuction twice, but each time I've gained back the weight. Every time I get near what could become an intimate relationship, I put the weight back on."

My patients have trained me to listen for the pain behind the words, so I guessed what he proceeded to tell me. When he was between the ages of eight and sixteen, an authority figure in his life had abused him.

He explained that he had difficulty forming intimate relationships, even though he wished he could have one. "Somehow this problem manifests itself as back pain, which is why I'm here," he concluded.

We discussed how the back pain was probably stemming from the tragic issues in his past. I asked him, "How can we organize the building blocks to help you with the heartache issues so that in the process, the back pain can diminish as well?"

As his next steps, we organized a plan that included seeing a nutritionist, continuing to see his psychologist, and coming to me to understand that his physical anatomy was actually in quite good condition. There were no herniated disks, no surgery needed—but he needed to hear from a pain specialist that his physical symptoms and his psychological symptoms went hand in hand. He needed information that legitimized his anatomy as normal while helping him understand the dynamics of how emotional conditions can manifest in physical ways. He already sensed that as his psychological health improved, his physical health would improve, but he needed it confirmed by a medical professional.

After the death of my daughter Ellie, I had recurring encounters with her in dreams. Although the dreams were not violent or sad in themselves, I would waken exhausted or disturbed. I saw a Jungian psychologist who helped me reframe the dreams. I no longer dread these visitations by Ellie. The elective decision to seek psychological treatment for the disturbing dreams has lessened the lingering heartache of losing a child. Now I actually look forward to the dreams in which the memory and spirit of Ellie are kept very much alive.

In time I have found myself open to new relationships while carrying the scars of the loss of Ellie. Paradoxically, the scars help me find a new rhythm to life. Now my slow, regular pulse is in marked contrast to the rapid, thready pulse I experienced during the acute phase of heartache or the faster pulse associated with a frenetic lifestyle from the past.

Ellie is in my heart, and so is the painful void of her absence not subject to evidence-based understanding, perhaps, but no less real than catecholamines. Here are some steps I have taken to move toward acceptance and renewal in my own life:

1. Recognize the gifts that Ellie gave to our family: She was the lighthearted member of a serious, goal-oriented family. Her humor and laid-back behavior were a good counterpoint to a highly focused and over-achieving family.
2. In the tragedy of loss, accept the mysteries that later may be more clearly revealed. Our understanding is limited to the here and now, but the future may reveal a deeper meaning for our significant life events.

3. Rest in the inner knowing that there will be insights gained from the pain of losing Ellie: I must learn to wait patiently and expectantly for such revelations.

4. Celebrate the funny stories and tender moments of our life together with her brother and sister and anticipate a continued story as the mystery of life and death evolves—in the same way that destructive forest fires germinate seeds that have lain dormant for years.

Returning to the house at Wolf Creek Pass in the full bloom of a Rocky Mountain summer, I sense the rhythms of nature surrounding me. Here, too, Ellie's spirit is very present. She was particularly exuberant at Wolf Creek, the hard work on the river restoration and the tree farm seemed effortless joy for her.

For the first year after Ellie's death, going to that house had left me feeling physically challenged by a lack of energy and a heavy heart. However, gradually there was a transformation. It is now a place of peace where I welcome vivid memories of her. When she was six years old, we planted a tiny blue spruce. It is now at least thirty feet tall, and it has two equally towering tops—a symbol of Ellie and me in step with the passing of time. Just beyond the tree I can see the West Fork of the San Juan River rumbling by on its way to form part of the Colorado River. I visualize its birth to the North in the Weminuche Wilderness and its dispersal of many life forms into the Pacific Ocean. I've seen the power of the high water from spring runoff, the peaceful meandering of the low flows in September and October, and the raging flash flood after a cloudburst. These changing rhythms mirror the flow of our lives, from birth to death—the turbulent times interspersed with periods of tranquility.

It is at Wolf Creek that the essence of Ellie is as close as my shadow. Here, I choose to talk to her and acknowledge her presence. Even though there are those poignant moments when Ellie seems like a distant memory, the rhythms of nature help keep alive the spirit of those who have gone before. It refuels the hope that at some point in time we will be reunited with loved ones whom the river has taken to the sea.

EPILOGUE

In the midst of the pain of acute heartache, I wonder about the power of technology that offers immediate contact with the world. Is there healing power in access to information and communication with others?

How can we develop an inward, prayer-filled listening? Our days are filled with media stimuli that keep us distracted in our waking hours and even in our dreams.

> The truth of the matter is we enjoy our technologic gluttony. It is so stimulating and interesting. [51]

We are taught daily—hourly—how much better and more efficient our lives are with improved communications by computers and e-mail, cell phones and text messaging, Twitter and Facebook, and other social and information networks. We are almost never instructed in silence and listening. How then do we practice and learn to go within for silence and balance in our noisy world?

---

51   Foster, Richard, *Sanctuary of the Soul, p. 104.*

How do we turn our thoughts inward? How do we use contemplation and silence?

A Quaker poem clearly speaks to the practice of silence:

> Teach me to stop and listen,
> Teach me to center down.
> Teach me the use of silence,
> Teach me where peace is found.
>
> Teach me to hear your calling,
> Teach me to search your word.
> Teach me to hear in silence,
> Things I have never heard.
>
> Teach me to be collected,
> Teach me to be in tune.
> Teach me to be directed,
> Silence will end so soon.
>
> Then when it's time for moving,
> Grant it that I might bring,
> To every day and moment,
> Peace from a silent spring.
>
> "Teach Me To Stop," Ken Medema
> (Waco, TX: Word Music, 1978)

But, in treating heartache, technology and silence are not mutually exclusive. They can be a powerful balance, even synergistic pairing, for identifying new resources and developing inner strength.

Because of the insights of broken heart syndrome, it is now easier for the medical establishment to recognize heartache and treat it proactively. My hope is that it is now easier for individuals to expect recovery from heartache instead of allowing it to define them. There is real hope, and real help, for bringing healing to some of the deepest wounds of the heart. And that is good news for us all.

Heartache is a shattering experience, but the fragments may come together to create a new kind of wholeness. In the moment we first glimpse this new vision of wholeness, we begin to heal our heartache.

INDEX

ACKNOWLEDGMENTS

A topic that includes scientific data as well as emotional and experiential information depends on many sources. I offer my gratitude to all those whose research and ideas support this work. Observing the challenges faced by my patients brought an added depth and compassion to this book. Practicing medicine with fine and dedicated physicians throughout my career offered me insights beyond my own experience.

I am particularly indebted to Kathy Helmers for her enthusiasm and dedication to this project. Her conceptual definition of the material, chapter organization, and wordsmithing talents made this a more articulate and readable book for its audience.

To the following friends and family who graciously agreed to read and review the manuscript, I extend my sincere thanks for your generosity: Pratap Avasthi, MD (nephrology) and Pushpa Avasthi, MD (pathology); Marilyn Butterstein, RN; Peg Cronin; Darren Dalton; Michelle Davis (psychology) and Fred Davis, MD (pain specialty); Marg Elliston; Richard Garbe, MD (anesthesiology); Al Goto; Susan Harper; Dick Hattan, MD (radiology) and Gail Hattan; Emily Hinds; Eric and Aleacia Hinds; Kochu Koshy, MD (cardiology) and Valsala

Koshy, MD (pathology); Shireen Jacob; Dick Lueker, MD (cardiology); Reza J. Mehran, MD (cardiovascular surgery); Pat McNab (counseling); Traci Mullins, RN; Steve Othling; Kevin Pauza, MD (spine intervention and physiatrist); Leslie Reynolds, RN; Rabbi Carolyn Silver; Ann Simon; Dora Tse Pe; Ann Tull; Revs. Roger and Libby Weber; Sara Voorhees; Joan Weissman; and Kiersten Yanni. Their feedback and careful edits were invaluable.

My copyeditor, Laura Burns, worked to bring this work together and gave it the final push for publication. I am very grateful for her fine-tuning of the final drafts of this book.

Made in the USA
San Bernardino, CA
24 June 2017